Common Core State Standards for Grade 7

Also by the Author

Common Core State Standards for Grades K–1: Language Arts Instructional Strategies and Activities

Common Core State Standards for Grades 2–3: Language Arts Instructional Strategies and Activities

Common Core State Standards for Grades 4–5: Language Arts Instructional Strategies and Activities

Common Core State Standards for Grade 6: Language Arts Instructional Strategies and Activities

Common Core State Standards for Grade 7

Language Arts Instructional Strategies and Activities

Michelle Manville

ROWMAN & LITTLEFIELD
Lanham • Boulder • New York • London

Published by Rowman & Littlefield
A wholly owned subsidiary of The Rowman & Littlefield Publishing Group, Inc.
4501 Forbes Boulevard, Suite 200, Lanham, Maryland 20706
www.rowman.com

16 Carlisle Street, London W1D 3BT, United Kingdom

Copyright © 2014 by Michelle Manville

All rights reserved. No part of this book may be reproduced in any form or by any electronic or mechanical means, including information storage and retrieval systems, without written permission from the publisher, except by a reviewer who may quote passages in a review.

British Library Cataloguing in Publication Information Available

Library of Congress Cataloging-in-Publication Data

Manville, Michelle, 1953–
Common core state standards for grade 7 : language arts instructional strategies and activities / Michelle Manville.
  pages cm
Includes bibliographical references.
ISBN 978-1-4758-1089-9 (pbk. : alk. paper)—ISBN 978-1-4758-1090-5 (electronic) 1. Language arts (Middle school)—Curricula—United States—States. 2. Language arts (Middle school)—Standards—United States—States. 3. Middle school education—Activity programs—United States. I. Title.
LB1631.M3854 2014
428.0071'2—dc23
2014003642

∞™ The paper used in this publication meets the minimum requirements of American National Standard for Information Sciences Permanence of Paper for Printed Library Materials, ANSI/NISO Z39.48-1992.

Printed in the United States of America

Contents

Introduction vii

1	Instructional Strategies and Activities: An Overview	1
2	Grade 7 Common Core State Standards	13
3	Grades 6–8 Text Exemplars	23
4	Grade 7 Strategies and Activities for Reading Literature	27
5	Grade 7 Strategies and Activities for Reading Informational Text	55
6	Grade 7 Strategies and Activities for Writing	81
7	Grade 7 Strategies and Activities for Speaking and Listening	99
8	Grade 7 Strategies and Activities for Language	105
9	Grade 7 Strategies and Activities for Reading Literacy in History and Social Studies	111
10	Grade 7 Strategies and Activities for Reading Literacy in Science and Technical Subjects	123
11	Grade 7 Strategies and Activities for Writing in History, Social Studies, Science and Technical Subjects	139

Appendix A: Summary Frames 149
Appendix B: Position Paper Format 151
Appendix C: Stem Questions 153
Appendix D: Hypothesis Worksheet 155
Appendix E: Primary Source Analysis 157
Appendix F: SMART Goals 159
Appendix G: Sample Grade 7 Advance Organizers 161
Appendix H: Sample Parent Letter 163
Appendix I: Products and Performances 165
Appendix J: Verbs to Question 167
References 171
About the Author 173

Introduction

The Common Core State Standards (CCSS) for English Language Arts and Literacy in History/Social Studies, Science, and Technical Subjects were developed to ensure that students are ready for the challenges of college and career literacy by the end of their high school years. The standards were developed around K–12 grade-specific areas of reading literature and informational text, writing, speaking and listening, and language. These research- and evidence-based standards are rigorous and are aligned to the College and Career Readiness anchor standards, which establish what all students should know and be able to do upon entering postsecondary institutions.

At a time when schools across the nation are looking for ways to improve student achievement in most content areas, it seems reasonable to combine the standards and effective instructional strategies as you create activities to help with the implementation of the CCSS.

When you look at the CCSS, think of the standards as representative of what students need to know and be able to do and what you need to do as a teacher to help them be successful. Based on the identified CCSS and other skills, students need to know how to compare and contrast, summarize information and take notes, create visual representations of information, work together collaboratively, conduct research, and be able to ask and answer higher-order questions. Additionally, to help students achieve success, teachers need to provide ample opportunities to practice new skills and demonstrate and enhance knew learning.

A multitude of studies have been conducted over the past thirty years. From these studies, Education Northwest, formerly Northwest Regional Education Laboratory (2005), compiled a list of effective instructional strategies with descriptions, research findings, and implementation suggestions. When developing activities to address CCSS, keep in mind the strategies of identifying similarities and differences, summarizing and note taking, nonlinguistic representations, cooperative learning, generating and testing hypotheses, questions, cues, and advanced organizers, and homework and practice. As teachers, provide many opportunities for homework and practice as you implement the CCSS.

There's no guarantee that activities based on any strategy will help in every instance, and it may be quite possible that some strategies are more effective in certain subject areas and grade levels and with students from different backgrounds and aptitudes. Whether or not you use a strategy will depend on your students' previous knowledge and current abilities.

It is the intent of this book to give teachers a ready-made resource to use when planning lessons around CCSS. In each section you will find grade-appropriate, ready-to-use activities aligned to specific CCSS in English Language Arts and Literacy in History/Social Studies, Science, and Technical Subjects. All you need to supply is the content-rich text.

It is my hope that you will find this an essential component of your instructional materials as you plan your curriculum for the students of the twenty-first century.

ONE
Instructional Strategies and Activities: An Overview

Many of the Common core State Standards (CCSS) can be taught and reinforced using a variety of activities combined with CCSS and effective instructional strategies. According to Visual Teaching Alliance (VTA) (www.visualteachingalliance.com), "approximately 65 percent of the population are visual learners" and "90 percent of the information that comes to the brain is visual." The VTA also states that "the brain processes visual information 60,000 times faster than text" and that "visual aids in the classroom improve learning by up to 400 percent."

The use of graphic organizers (i.e., visuals) enables students to better organize their thinking and gives a visual frame of reference for information. Students are able to see the connections between previous learning and new knowledge. Graphic organizers increase students' abilities to use higher-order thinking skills, facilitate retention of information, are very brain-friendly, and appeal to the multiple intelligences of visual-spatial, verbal-linguistic, logical-mathematical, and naturalist. The use of graphic organizers also helps those students who are English as a second language (ESL) or English language (EL) learners comprehend concepts more easily as there are fewer words to comprehend.

When you write lesson plans, think about the various graphic organizers you can use in activities: T-charts, Venn diagrams, matrices, concept maps, word webs, mind maps, graphs, chains, flowcharts, and lists. Several suggestions are given throughout this book, but you may find a different organizer to help you help your students link new information to old or organize thoughts. Not all organizers are age or grade appropriate so choose carefully.

For those standards that are not appropriate for graphic organizers, you will find suggestions for a wide variety of structures that you can use in your classrooms. The ideas you find do not represent a definitive list and you may adapt those suggestions to use in other instances.

The instructional strategies described on the next few pages have been identified as effective practices by various educational practitioners based on a multitude of research. *Common Core State Standards for Grade 7: Language Arts Instructional Strategies and Activities* addresses the use of these strategies with respect to the K–12 CCSS for English Language Arts and Literacy in History/Social Studies, Science, and Technical Subjects and provides a multitude of ready-to-use activities.

SIMILARITIES AND DIFFERENCES

When students identify similarities and differences, the process helps students deepen the understanding of what they are learning. According to Markman and Gentner (1996), identifying similarities and differences is a basic cognitive process. Students use the processes of comparing, classifying, creating metaphors, and creating analogies to describe how items, events, processes, or concepts are similar or different. Comparison and contrast activities help students to better comprehend new concepts and allows the connection of new knowledge to existing concepts.

Teachers should not only point out similarities and differences to students, but should also allow students to develop their own strategies for comparing similarities and differences (http://netc.org/focus/strategies/iden.php). Students in Grade 7 should also describe *how* compared elements are different. T-charts and Venn diagrams are effective tools for teachers and students to identify similarities and differences. Matrices can also illustrate these concepts.

Grade 7 Activities

Activities to identify similarities and differences include creating T-charts, two- and three-circle Venn diagrams, organizational charts, classification charts, lists, graphs, maps, summary frames, essays, short research projects, opinion writing, creating analogies, mind maps, or word webs.

SUMMARIZING AND TAKING NOTES

Summarizing occurs unconsciously for most of us; yet, ask students to write a summary of a chapter or a story and they may complain it is too difficult. We need to teach students to give us only the important details—eliminating the trivialities not necessary for comprehension. Valerie Anderson and Suzanne Hidi synthesized various research on summarization. According to Anderson and Hidi (1998/1999), when you first begin teaching summarization, be sure to choose short excerpts with easy text, such as narratives or texts with familiar concepts and ideas. Anderson and Hidi (1998/1999) also indicate that students need to be able to select or delete what is included and then reduce the information into a manageable amount.

Summary Frames

The use of summary frames helps students select and reduce information for summaries using specific questions and helps students develop a deeper comprehension of the information read. A summary frame is an effective structure when summarizing reading assignments. Studies by Meyer and Freedle (1984) show that reading comprehension increases when students learn how to incorporate summary frames. Summary frames also help students to focus on important information and allow teachers to determine the depth of comprehension through student responses.

Narrative or story frames include information about the characters, setting, actions, feelings and goals of the main character, and the consequences.

Definition frames use four questions: (1) What concept is being defined? (2) To which category does the item belong? (3) What are the attributes or characteristics of the concept? (4) What examples are given to illustrate the concept?

Problem-solution frames introduce a problem and identify one or more solutions following this format: statement of something that happened or might happen that could be problematic, a description of a solution, statements of other possible solutions, identification of a solution with the greatest chance of success.

Questions in an argumentation frame are centered on the information that leads to a claim, the basic statement of focus, examples that support the claim, and concessions made about the claim. You will need to know the abilities of your students to begin using the argumentation frame effectively in your classroom.

Grade 7 Activities

Common summarization activities for Grade 7 include the use of narrative, or story, definition, and problem-solution summary frames, acrostics, journal entries, visual representations (bulletin boards, posters, models), concept webs, multicolumn T-charts, concept webs, timelines, outlines, 5W and How charts, raps or other songs, mnemonics, and paraphrases. See Appendix A for examples of summary frames.

Taking Notes

The concept of taking notes in class previously implied writing every important word one could remember as quickly as possible or copying the teacher's words from the blackboard, whiteboard, or overhead projector. If we all had photographic memories, then there would be no reason to take notes. However, that is not the case. The good news is that students can be taught how to summarize information and take good notes.

Verbatim notes are the least effective way of taking notes in a classroom setting and are not conducive to selecting and reducing, which is key to taking good notes. When copying the teacher's words, students are not engaged in the information except to the extent that they write down every word. Very little, if anything, is committed to long-term or, even short-term, memory. Students must identify the key information they are learning about and put it into their own words.

Taking notes is very personal in style, but students need to be taught various formats to enable them to choose the style that best suits their tastes and needs. Teachers should model good note-taking formats. Begin with outlines of information you are going to present. Impress upon students that reviewing and revising notes can lead to a deeper understanding of the information presented and will help the students to make the information their own (Anderson & Armbruster, 1986).

Grade 7 Activities

Activities to teach note taking include creating graphic organizers, outlines, note cards, paraphrases, mnemonic devices, concept maps, flashcards, two-column notes, flowcharts, multicolumn charts, and diagrams. Other activities include reading or taking notes outside or in a special place in the classroom, using content-related visuals in the classroom, and creating songs or pictures that represent key concepts.

NONLINGUISTIC REPRESENTATIONS

When students use nonlinguistic representations in activities, they use words, pictures, and symbols to convey knowledge while learning. The use of this strategy helps students synthesize information in a way that makes sense to them and are then better able to retain and recall the information. In most classroom applications, students and teachers will combine words in graphic organizers with the nonlinguistic representations. The use of visual representations helps students recognize how concepts are connected (National Council of Teachers of Mathematics, 2000).

There are many examples of mind maps, webs, or pictorial representations you can use in the classroom. You may have to teach students how to create these representations. Kagan and Kagan (1997) offers these helpful hints when creating mind maps: "use white space, practice symbols and images, emphasize important images, and practice." Students can also create pictographs that use representative pictures or symbols to present information.

The brain is a pattern-seeking device; nonlinguistic representations are patterns. Use of these patterns can help most students, especially the visual-spatial student, comprehend and retain information. The use of patterns helps students organize their thinking and helps them apply what they have learned (Bransford et al., 1999; Lehrer & Chazen, 1998).

Nonlinguistic representation activities create visuals, and according to Lehrer and Chazen (1998, p. 6) "by ignoring visualization, curricula not only fail to engage a powerful part of students' minds in service of their mathematical thinking, but also fail to develop students' skills at visual exploration and argument." The ability to visualize can also serve the language arts student as well.

Grade 7 Activities

To create activities using nonlinguistic representations, include role-playing and dramatizations such as plays or skits, puppet shows, press conferences; create murals, brochures, bulletin boards, posters, or scenic backdrops; illustrate favorite parts of stories or poems or create bookmarks or book covers; participate in kinesthetic activities; produce oral readings, recordings, narrations and recitations; listen to commercially produced CDs or student recordings; create physical models such as dioramas or representative artifacts; and draw and create other pictorial representations such as illustrated webs, murals, dioramas, trifolds, scrapbooks, posters, T-shirts, book jackets or bookmarks, mind maps, travel brochures, and PowerPoint presentations.

COOPERATIVE LEARNING

A graphic attributed to American psychologist William Glasser, based on a graphic created by Edgar Dale (1969, p. 108), indicates: We learn 10 percent of what we read, 20 percent of what we hear, 30 percent of what we see, 50 percent of what we see and hear, 70 percent of what we discuss, 80 percent of what we experience, and 95 percent of what we teach to others. Perhaps an easier way to describe Glasser's view of learning would be to say "two heads are better than one."

What Is Cooperative Learning?

Cooperative learning is *not* group work. It *is* where two or more students work together cooperatively to achieve a common goal. According to Johnson and Johnson (1999) (as cited in Education Northwest, formerly Northwest Regional Educational Laboratory, 2005, para. 1) "effective cooperative learning occurs when students work together to accomplish shared goals and when positive structures are in place to support that process." Students in Grade 7 should continue to work with others as the concept of cooperative learning is a lifelong lesson that will help them throughout their lives.

Teachers and students alike are often placed into group settings where either everyone or no one is in charge; where chaos reigns; where nothing is accomplished. Unless you know how to work in a group, the group is almost certainly doomed. When groups work within specific guidelines, then the group allows for more student interaction, inquiry thinking, time-on-task, in-depth questions, and student accountability. Shy students will feel safe. Studies show that cooperative learning enhances student performance and should not be based on competition.

A Teacher's Role in Cooperative Learning

The teacher's role in cooperative learning includes selecting the group size, assignment of students to the groups, arranging the classroom, providing appropriate materials, setting the task and goal structure, monitoring student-student interaction, intervening to solve problems and teach skills, and evaluating the outcomes (Johnson & Johnson, 1999).

Sometimes teachers will want to assign specific roles to specific students or you may want to give a list of possible roles to students and let them work it out. You will always want to make sure that roles rotate among the students. The number of roles you have will obviously depend on the number of students in a group and the nature of the work to be done in the group. You might want to create roles such as leader, recorder or secretary, checker, speaker, facilitator, timekeeper, summarizer, and reflector (http://serc.carleton.edu/introgeo/cooperative/roles.html).

Grade 7 Activities

Cooperative learning activities for Grade 7 include the Kagan Cooperative Learning (Kagan & Kagan, 1997) structures of Think-Pair-Share, Paraphrase Passport, and Jigsaw. Other activities include peer editing and revising, conducting group research, publishing, collaborative discussions, and group presentations.

GENERATING AND TESTING HYPOTHESES

Students must learn to question in order to question to learn. Students who are able to generate and test their hypotheses—ask questions and explain their hypotheses—will greatly enhance their own learning. Children begin to ask questions as soon as they begin talking and continue to ask questions through adulthood. Teachers can help students learn to ask good questions which will help them make better hypotheses. Students who are able to explain their hypotheses will demonstrate their understanding of concepts as well.

Research Findings

According to Lavoie and Good (1998) and Lawson (1998) (as cited in Education Northwest, formerly Northwest Regional Educational Laboratory, 2005, para. 3) "understanding increases when students are asked to explain the scientific principles they are working from and the hypotheses they generate from these principles."

Similarly, White and Frederickson (1998) (as cited in Education Northwest, formerly Northwest Regional Educational Laboratory, 2005, para. 5) found that when comparing "inquiry-based instruction and traditional teaching methods (such as lectures and textbook-based instruction), researchers found that inquiry methods helped students gain a better understanding of fundamental science concepts." These ideas can be applied to language arts, too.

Applications for Language Arts Classrooms

The ability to generate and test hypotheses isn't just for science anymore. For example, a language arts teacher could ask students to read literature, predict the actions of one or more of the characters, and then read and discuss the accuracy of the predictions (Kuhn, 2009). Leach (2010) describes how teachers show students various pictures dealing with short stories or novels they are reading and how teachers ask students to predict the outcome of events based on the pictures.

Students can predict the ending of a story at the middle of the book and discuss the accuracy of their hypotheses at the end. Other ways to generate and test hypotheses include learning about a debatable historical event and hypothesizing about the actual events, reading two or more books to test the hypothesis; brainstorming techniques that persuade people in debate and hypothesizing which techniques work best; and finally, talking about how characters in a novel react and hypothesizing about how students would react in the same situation, checking with several to test the hypothesis (Janel W., 2009).

Seize the opportunity to use the natural curiosity of all students. They love to question why we do things, so turn it around on them and let them discover why and what. Teach students the art of asking strong, higher-order questions, and challenge them to explain the results of their findings.

Grade 7 Activities

Classroom activities for generating and testing hypotheses in Grade 7 include asking students to make and test hypotheses, make predictions, solve problems, conduct historical investigations, make observations, and make decisions based on information. See Appendix C for stem questions and Appendix J for lists of higher- and lower-order verbs.

QUESTIONS, CUES, AND ADVANCE ORGANIZERS

The brain as a pattern-seeking device looks to link new information to previous knowledge. When we use cues, questions, and advance organizers, we access what students already know and prepare them for what they are about to learn.

Research Findings

Marzano et al. (2001, p. 113) found (as cited in Davis & Tinsley, 1967; Fillippone, 1998) that "cueing and questioning might account for as much as 80 percent of what occurs in a given classroom on a given day." If we are asking that many questions, then we need to consider the quality of the questions we ask. Are we asking questions that reflect the most important content? Do we ask higher-order questions or do we simply ask students to recall information?

Redfield and Rousseau (1981) found that asking higher-level questions, rather than asking recall questions, requires students to analyze information which results in more learning. Do teachers tend to ask more lower-order questions? Do we use questions, cues, and advance organizers to focus learning? Are we waiting long enough for students to give more thoughtful responses? Do we give some students longer to respond because of who they are? T. W. Fowler (1975) found that when teachers are taught a technique related to the amount of wait time after asking a question, students are more likely to participate and participate more frequently in small group student-to-student interactions.

Determine the Types of Questions Asked

One way to determine the types of questions you use in the classroom is to audio record several instructional sessions in your classroom. This will give you the opportunity to hear how much wait time you give and to whom. Using the "Verbs to Question" page in Appendix J, mark the verbs you use in your class. If you use more lower-order verbs in instruction, then use more higher-order verbs. If you teach more than one content area, you might want to tape various content areas and see what types of questions you ask. Maybe there is a correlation to the content area where you ask the higher- or lower-order questions.

You can also create a list of higher-order, grade-appropriate verbs and post them in your classroom. You may wish to choose verbs from Appendix J. When you use KWL charts, use the list to help improve the questions on your chart. If we do not use higher-order questions in our classroom instruction, then we cannot expect students to ask them either.

Use Cues and Questions

Cues are hints or reminders that help access prior knowledge and are generally explicit in nature. In the book *Checking for Understanding: Formative Assessment Techniques for Your Classroom*, Douglas Fisher and Nancy Frey (2007) suggest teachers use symbols, words, or phrases to help students recall information. Fisher and Frey (2007) also suggest using direct eye contact, facial expressions, body posture, physical distance, silence, short verbal acknowledgments, and sub-summaries (restating or paraphrasing main ideas).

Questions can act as cues or require students to analyze information. Questions should engage students in their learning and increase participation in the classroom. Fisher and Frey (2007) identified several strategies that are helpful in questioning. These strategies include response cards, hand signals, and audience response systems.

Advance Organizers

Sometimes you need more than a cue or question. Use advance organizers when introducing new concepts as they will help link previous knowledge to the new learning that is going to take place. Advance organizers are organizational frameworks that provide guidance as to the important information in a lesson or unit. Information that is presented graphically and symbolically reinforces reading and learning skills (Brookbank et al., 1999).

Grade 7 Activities

When creating Grade 7 activities around questions, cues and advance organizers include the use of higher-order questions, using visual cues and advance organizers such as narrative frames, timelines, and webs. See Appendix G for sample Grade 7 advance organizers.

HOMEWORK AND PRACTICE

Thomas Edison once said that "genius is 2 percent inspiration and 98 percent perspiration" and he felt that hard work would get one to the "top rung of Fortune's ladder" (Jones, 1908, p. 347). It is up to us to make homework and practice meaningful to students so that their 98 percent perspiration will help them become the geniuses they can be. Create a variety of activities that enable students to practice the CCSS skills.

Homework activities should not be busy work. The activities should have a purpose that is clearly articulated to students. In the book, *Rethinking Homework: Best Practices That Support Diverse Needs*, Cathy Vatterott (2009) suggests homework be given to help the learning process in four ways: prelearning, checking for understanding, practice, and processing. It is important to prepare students for new content and for teachers to find out what students already know about the content.

Additionally, "students should easily understand the value of the task or be told explicitly how it [homework] helps learning" (Vatterott, 2009, p. 100). Give students specific reasons for the day's homework either in writing on the assignment itself or verbally. Use statements such as: today's homework will allow you to practice previous knowledge or new skills; reflect on learning; review for tests or quizzes; check for understanding of concepts (Vatterott, 2009).

There is an old adage that says "practice makes perfect." However, many believe practice makes better and that only perfect practice makes perfect. The very essence of homework is to provide such practice, especially for rote skills—alphabet, multiplication tables, the names of all the state capitals in the United States. But if students do not understand a concept and teachers do not check for understanding, then the practice could lead to misconceptions and inaccurate learning.

Thomas Armstrong (2006, p. 129) suggests teachers "link [homework] in some way to the feelings, memories, or personal associations of the students" with words such as "think of a time in your life when you." Whenever you connect the curriculum to students in such a manner, you create an emotionally meaningful attachment between the student and the curriculum.

Research Findings and Recommendations

According to Harris Cooper (1989, p. 89) "it is better to distribute material across several assignments rather than have homework concentrate only on material covered in class that day." Students need to process new information as they link it to previous knowledge. Processing is where students reflect on concepts by considering specific questions to ask, applying information learned, and making connections to a bigger picture (Vatterott, 2009).

You will also want to consider the amount of homework and practice activities at each grade level. Recommendations from various studies by the Pennsylvania Department of Education (1973), Bond and Smith (1966), and Strang (1975) (as cited in Marzano et al., 2001) for total minutes of homework per day vary from forty to ninety minutes for middle school. Other schools of thought use the "ten-minute rule" to establish optimum homework amounts. Cooper ("Duke Study: Homework," 2006) described it as ten minutes of homework per grade level. Additional studies show that about every thirty minutes of "additional" homework students do per night their grade point average increases about half a point (Keith & Cool, 1992).

In her article "The War on Homework," Bea McGarvey (2007, p. 6) "advised educators to ask how homework supports the knowledge they want students to learn." She also asks teachers to look at their grade books to see if they are tracking assignments or attainment of learning goals. Are your homework and practice activities geared toward learning or keeping students busy?

Suggestions for Parents

For those parents who absolutely "must" help, give them a list of "helpful activities" in which they can participate without jeopardizing procedures and processes you have established and content you have taught in class. A good time to share tips with parents could be at an open house or back-to-school night. Teachers could also include a list of tips in registration packets that may be handed or sent out just before the new school year.

How should middle school parents help their children with homework? Parents can help the child find a quiet location to do homework; establish a sense of organization by creating a homework supply box that contains paper, pens, pencils, tape, glue, dictionary/thesaurus, calculator, markers, rulers, and other necessary items; establish a time or schedule for homework; have a positive attitude about the homework and check it for completion and understanding.

Parents can work with students to create mnemonics to help remember key details. Prepare Q&As—where a parent creates questions over the material and the student reads to find the answers. Encourage parents to participate in "quick writes," where the student reads or reviews small chunks of notes or material and then shares, either verbally or in writing on sticky notes, any key details. The parent can check the notes or material for accuracy, and the student can add the sticky notes to the study materials. Students can use their notes and other materials to "teach" concepts to parents.

Students can share their homework assignments with their parents so the students see that parents value the time and effort and learning that go along with homework. When students see that the work they do is valued, then possibly they are more inclined to do better work.

Grade 7 Activities

Homework and practice activities for Grade 7 include summary frames, advertisements, museum exhibits, recitations, quiz shows, flashcards, webs, journal writing, scavenger hunts, Venn diagrams, charts and graphs, timelines, speeches, scrapbooks, letters to authors or speakers, keyboarding skills, various forms of writing, Q&A sessions, bio-poems, research projects, read-alouds, note cards, news stories and headlines, poetry, storyboards, concept webs, and many others. See Appendix H for a sample parent letter.

LET'S GET STARTED!

Now you have an overview of various instructional strategies and activities to use with the Grade 7 CCSS. The rest of the book is devoted to specific activities to use with the strands of reading literature, reading informational text, writing, speaking and listening, and language. You also have strategies and activities for reading literacy and writing in history, social studies, science, and technical subjects. Within each strand you will find many ready-to-use grade level appropriate activities aligned to specific standards. Many activities will incorporate other standards as well.

You will also find a list of the grade level text exemplars; you are not expected to use the exemplars, but if you have them in your classroom, use them. There are many other wonderful, grade-appropriate books for you and your students to use if the exemplars are not available to you. Other selections are suggested within the activities.

I hope you find this a valuable tool as you implement the CCSS in your classroom.

TWO
Grade 7 Common Core State Standards

READING LITERATURE

- RL.7.1—Cite several pieces of textual evidence to support analysis of what the text says explicitly as well as inferences drawn from the text.
- RL.7.2—Determine a theme or central idea of a text and analyze its development over the course of the text; provide an objective summary of the text.
- RL.7.3—Analyze how particular elements of a story or drama interact (e.g., how setting shapes the characters or plot).
- RL.7.4—Determine the meaning of words and phrases as they are used in a text, including figurative and connotative meanings; analyze the impact rhymes and other repetitions of sounds (e.g., alliteration) on a specific verse or stanza of a poem or section of a story or drama.
- RL.7.5—Analyze how a drama's or poem's form or structure (e.g., soliloquy, sonnet) contributes to its meaning.
- RL.7.6—Analyze how an author develops and contrasts the points of view of different characters or narrators in a text.
- RL.7.7—Compare and contrast a written story, drama, or poem to its audio, filmed, staged, or multimedia version, analyzing the effects of techniques unique to each medium (e.g., lighting, sound, color, or camera focus and angles in a film).
- RL.7.9—Compare and contrast a fictional portrayal of a time, place, or character and a historical account of the same period as a means of understanding how authors of fiction use or alter history.

- RL.7.10—By the end of the year, read and comprehend literature, including stories, dramas, and poems, in the Grades 6–8 text complexity band proficiently, with scaffolding as needed at the high end of the range.

READING INFORMATIONAL TEXTS

- RI.7.1—Cite several pieces of textual evidence to support analysis of what the text says explicitly as well as inferences drawn from the text.
- RI.7.2—Determine two or more central ideas in a text and analyze their development over the course of the text; provide an objective summary of the text.
- RI.7.3—Analyze the interactions between individuals, events, and ideas in a text (e.g., how ideas influence individuals or events, or how individuals influence ideas or events).
- RI.7.4—Determine the meaning of words and phrases as they are used in a text, including figurative, connotative, and technical meanings; analyze the impact of a specific word choice on meaning and tone.
- RI.7.5—Analyze the structure an author uses to organize a text, including how the major sections contribute to the whole and to the development of ideas.
- RI.7.6—Determine an author's point of view or purpose in a text and analyze how the author distinguishes his or her position from that of others.
- RI.7.7—Compare and contrast a text to an audio, video, or multimedia version of the text, analyzing each medium's portrayal of the subject (e.g., how the delivery of a speech affects the impact of the words).
- RI.7.8—Trace and evaluate the argument and specific claims in a text, assessing whether the reasoning is sound and the evidence is relevant and sufficient to support the claims.
- RI.7.9—Analyze how two or more authors writing about the same topic shape their presentations of key information by emphasizing different evidence or advancing different interpretations of facts.
- RI.7.10—By the end of the year, read and comprehend literary nonfiction in the Grades 6–8 text complexity band proficiently, with scaffolding as needed at the high end of the range.

WRITING

- W.7.1—Write arguments to support claims with clear reasons and relevant evidence.

- W.7.1a—Introduce claim(s), acknowledge alternate or opposing claims, and organize the reasons and evidence logically.
- W.7.1b—Support claim(s) with logical reasoning and relevant evidence, using accurate, credible sources and demonstrating an understanding of the topic or text.
- W.7.1c—Use words, phrases, and clauses to create cohesion and clarify the relationships among claim(s), reasons, and evidence.
- W.7.1d—Establish and maintain a formal style.
- W.7.1e—Provide a concluding statement or section that follows from and supports the argument presented.
- W.7.2—Write informative/explanatory texts to examine a topic and convey ideas, concepts, and information through the selection, organization, and analysis of relevant content.
- W.7.2a—Introduce a topic clearly, previewing what is to follow; organize ideas, concepts, and information using strategies such as definition, classification, comparison/contrast, and cause/effect; include formatting (e.g., headings), graphics (e.g., charts, tables), and multimedia when useful to aiding comprehension.
- W.7.2b—Develop the topic with relevant facts, definitions, concrete details, quotations, or other information and examples.
- W.7.2c—Use appropriate transitions to create cohesion and clarify the relationships among ideas and concepts.
- W.7.2d—Use precise language and domain-specific vocabulary to inform about or explain the topic.
- W.7.2e—Establish and maintain a formal style.
- W.7.2f—Provide a concluding statement or section that follows from and supports the information or explanation presented.
- W.7.3—Write narratives to develop real or imagined experiences or events using effective technique, relevant descriptive details, and well-structured event sequences.
- W.7.3a—Engage and orient the reader by establishing a context and point of view and introducing a narrator and/or characters; organize an event sequence that unfolds naturally and logically.
- W.7.3b—Use narrative techniques, such as dialogue, pacing, and description, to develop experiences, events, and/or characters.
- W.7.3c—Use a variety of transition words, phrases, and clauses to convey sequence and signal shifts from one time frame or setting to another.
- W.7.3d—Use precise words and phrases, relevant descriptive details, and sensory language to capture the action and convey experiences and events.
- W.7.3e—Provide a conclusion that follows from and reflects on the narrated experiences or events.

- W.7.4—Produce clear and coherent writing in which the development, organization, and style are appropriate to task, purpose, and audience.
- W.7.5—With some guidance and support from peers and adults, develop and strengthen writing as needed by planning, revising, editing, rewriting, or trying a new approach, focusing on how well purpose and audience have been addressed.
- W.7.6—Use technology, including the Internet, to produce and publish writing and link to and cite sources as well as to interact and collaborate with others, including linking to and citing sources.
- W.7.7—Conduct short research projects to answer a question, drawing on several sources and generating additional related, focused questions for further research and investigation.
- W.7.8—Gather relevant information from multiple print and digital sources, using search terms effectively; assess the credibility and accuracy of each source; and quote or paraphrase the data and conclusions of others while avoiding plagiarism and following a standard format for citation.
- W.7.9—Draw evidence from literary or informational texts to support analysis, reflection, and research.
- W.7.10—Write routinely over extended time frames (time for research, reflection, and revision) and shorter time frames (a single sitting or a day or two) for a range of discipline-specific tasks, purposes, and audiences.

SPEAKING AND LISTENING

- SL.7.1—Engage effectively in a range of collaborative discussions (one-on-one, in groups, and teacher led) with diverse partners on Grade 7 topics, texts, and issues, building on others' ideas and expressing their own clearly.
- SL.7.1a—Come to discussions prepared, having read or researched material under study; explicitly draw on that preparation by referring to evidence on the topic, text, or issue to probe and reflect on ideas under discussion.
- SL.7.1b—Follow rules for collegial discussions, track progress toward specific goals and deadlines, and define individual roles as needed.
- SL.7.1c—Pose questions that elicit elaboration and respond to others' questions and comments with relevant observations and ideas that bring the discussion back on topic as needed.
- SL.7.1d—Acknowledge new information expressed by others and, when warranted, modify their own views.

- SL.7.2—Analyze the main ideas and supporting details presented in diverse media and formats (e.g., visually, quantitatively, orally) and explain how the ideas clarify a topic, text, or issue under study.
- SL.7.3—Delineate a speaker's argument and specific claims, evaluating the soundness of the reasoning and the relevance and sufficiency of the evidence.
- SL.7.4—Present claims and findings, emphasizing salient points in a focused, coherent manner with pertinent descriptions, facts, details, and examples; use appropriate eye contact, adequate volume, and clear pronunciation.
- SL.7.5—Include multimedia components and visual displays in presentations to clarify claims and findings and emphasize salient points.
- SL.7.6—Adapt speech to a variety of contexts and tasks, demonstrating command of formal English when indicated or appropriate.

LANGUAGE

- L.7.1—Demonstrate command of the conventions of standard English grammar and usage when writing or speaking.
- L.7.1a—Explain the function of phrases and clauses in general and their function in specific sentences.
- L.7.1b—Choose among simple, compound, complex and compound-complex sentences to signal differing relationships among ideas.
- L.7.1c—Place phrases and clauses within a sentence, recognizing and correcting misplaced and dangling modifiers.
- L.7.2—Demonstrate command of the conventions of standard English capitalization, punctuation, and spelling when writing.
- L.7.2a—Use a comma to separate coordinate adjectives (e.g., "It was a fascinating, enjoyable movie" not "He wore an old[,]green shirt").
- L.7.2b—Spell correctly.
- L.7.3—Use knowledge of language and its conventions when writing, speaking, reading, or listening.
- L.7.3a—Choose language that expresses ideas precisely and concisely, recognizing and eliminating wordiness and redundancy.
- L.7.4—Determine or clarify the meaning of unknown and multiple-meaning words and phrases based on Grade 7 reading and content, choosing flexibly from a range of strategies.
- L.7.4a—Use context (e.g., the overall meaning of a sentence or paragraph; a word's position or function in a sentence) as a clue to the meaning of a word or phrase.

- L.7.4b—Use common, grade-appropriate Greek or Latin affixes and roots as clues to the meaning of a word (e.g., belligerent, bellicose, rebel).
- L.7.4c—Consult general and specialized reference materials (e.g., dictionaries, glossaries, thesauruses), both print and digital, to find the pronunciation of a word or determine or clarify its precise meaning or its part of speech.
- L.7.4d—Verify the preliminary determination of the meaning of a word or phrase (e.g., by checking the inferred meaning in context or in a dictionary).
- L.7.5—Demonstrate understanding of figurative language, word relationships, and nuances in word meanings.
- L.7.5a—Interpret figures of speech (e.g., literary, biblical, and mythological allusions) in context.
- L.7.5b—Use the relationship between particular words (e.g., synonym/antonym, analogy) to better understand each of the words.
- L.7.5c—Distinguish among the connotations (associations) of words with similar denotations (definitions) (e.g., refined, respectful, polite, diplomatic, condescending).
- L.7.6—Acquire and use accurately grade-appropriate general academic and domain-specific words and phrases; gather vocabulary knowledge when considering a word or phrase important to comprehension or expression.

READING LITERACY IN HISTORY/SOCIAL STUDIES

- RLHS.6-8.1—Cite specific textual evidence to support analysis of primary and secondary sources.
- RLHS.6-8.2—Determine the central ideas or information of a primary or secondary source; provide an accurate summary of the source distinct from prior knowledge or opinions.
- RLHS.6-8.3—Identify key steps in a text's description of a process related to history/social studies (e.g., how a bill becomes law, how interest rates are raised or lowered).
- RLHS.6-8.4—Determine the meaning of words and phrases as they are used in a text, including vocabulary specific to domains related to history/social studies.
- RLHS.6-8.5—Describe how a text presents information (e.g., sequentially, comparatively, causally).
- RLHS.6-8.6—Identify aspects of a text that reveal an author's point of view or purpose (e.g., loaded language, inclusion or avoidance of particular facts).

- RLHS.6-8.7—Integrate visual information (e.g., in charts, graphs, photographs, videos, or maps) with other information in print and digital texts.
- RLHS.6-8.8—Distinguish among fact, opinion, and reasoned judgment in a text.
- RLHS.6-8.9—Analyze the relationship between a primary and secondary source on the same topic.
- RLHS.6-8.10—By the end of the year, read and comprehend literature, including stories, dramas, and poems in the Grades 6–8 text complexity band proficiently, with scaffolding as needed at the high end of the range.

READING LITERACY IN SCIENCE AND TECHNICAL SUBJECTS

- RLST.6-8.1—Cite specific textual evidence to support analysis of science and technical texts.
- RLST.6-8.2—Determine the central ideas or conclusions of a text; provide an accurate summary of the text distinct from prior knowledge or opinions.
- RLST.6-8.3—Follow precisely a multistep procedure when carrying out experiments, taking measurements, or performing technical tasks.
- RLST.6-8.4—Determine the meaning of symbols, key terms, and other domain-specific words and phrases as they are used in a specific scientific or technical context relevant to Grades 6–8 texts and topics.
- RLST.6-8.5—Analyze the structure an author uses to organize a text, including how the major sections contribute to the whole and to an understanding of the topic.
- RLST.6-8.6—Analyze the author's purpose in providing an explanation, describing a procedure or discussing an experiment in a text.
- RLST.6-8.7—Integrate quantitative or technical information expressed in words in a text with a version of that information expressed visually (e.g., in a flowchart, diagram, model, graph, or table).
- RLST.6-8.8—Distinguish among facts, reasoned judgment based on research findings, and speculation in a text.
- RLST.6-8.9—Compare and contrast the information gained from experiments, simulations, video, or multimedia sources with that gained from reading a text on the same topic.
- RLST.6-8.10—By the end of the year, read and comprehend literary nonfiction in the Grades 6–8 text complexity band proficiently, with scaffolding as needed at the high end of the range.

WRITING LITERACY IN HISTORY/SOCIAL STUDIES, SCIENCE, AND TECHNICAL SUBJECTS

- WHST.6-8.1—Write arguments focused on discipline-specific content.
- WHST.6-8.1a—Introduce claim(s) about a topic or issue, acknowledge and distinguish the claim(s) from alternate or opposing claims, and organize the reasons and evidence logically.
- WHST.6-8.1b—Support claim(s) with logical reasoning and relevant, accurate data and evidence that demonstrate an understanding of the topic or text, using credible sources.
- WHST.6-8.1c—Use words, phrases, and clauses to create cohesion and clarify the relationships among claim(s), counterclaims, reasons, and evidence.
- WHST.6-8.1d—Establish and maintain a formal style.
- WHST.6-8.1e—Provide a concluding statement or section that follows from and supports the argument presented.
- WHST.6-8.2—Write informative/explanatory texts, including the narration of historical events, scientific procedures/experiments, or technical processes.
- WHST.6-8.2a—Introduce a topic clearly, previewing what is to follow; organize ideas, concepts, and information into broader categories as appropriate to achieving purpose; include formatting (e.g., headings), graphics (e.g., charts, tables), and multimedia when useful to aiding comprehension.
- WHST.6-8.2b—Develop the topic with relevant, well-chosen facts, definitions, concrete details, quotations, or other information and examples.
- WHST.6-8.2c—Use appropriate and varied transitions to create cohesion and clarify the relationships among ideas and concepts.
- WHST.6-8.2d—Use precise language and domain-specific vocabulary to inform about or explain the topic.
- WHST.6-8.2e—Establish and maintain a formal style and objective tone.
- WHST.6-8.2f—Provide a concluding statement or section that follows from and supports the information or explanation presented.
- WHST.6-8.4—Provide clear and coherent writing in which the development, organization, and style are appropriate to task, purpose, and audience.
- WHST.6-8.5—With some guidance and support from peers and adults, develop and strengthen writing as needed by planning, revising, editing, rewriting, or trying a new approach, focusing on how well purpose and audience have been addressed.

- WHST.6-8.6—Use technology, including the Internet, to produce and publish writing and present the relationships between information and ideas clearly and efficiently.
- WHST.6-8.7—Conduct short research projects to answer a question (including a self-generated question), drawing on several sources and generating additional related, focused questions that allow for multiple avenues of exploration.
- WHST.6-8.8—Gather relevant information from multiple print and digital sources, using search terms effectively; assess the credibility and accuracy of each source; and quote or paraphrase the data and conclusions of others while avoiding plagiarism and following a standard format for citation.
- WHST.6-8.9—Draw evidence from informational texts to support analysis, reflection, and research.
- WHST.6-8.10—Write routinely over extended time frames (time for reflection and revision) and shorter time frames (a single sitting or a day or two) for a range of discipline-specific tasks, purposes, and audiences.

NOTE

A complete list of text standards, exemplars, and resource materials as identified by the National Governors Association Center for Best Practices can be found at http://corestandards.org/ELA-Literacy.

THREE
Grades 6–8 Text Exemplars

STORIES

Alcott, Louisa May. *Little Women*
Cisneros, Sandra. "Eleven"
Cooper, Susan. *The Dark Is Rising*
Hamilton, Virginia. "The People Could Fly"
L'Engle, Madeleine. *A Wrinkle in Time*
Paterson, Katherine. *The Tale of the Mandarin Ducks*
Sutcliff, Rosemary. *Black Ships before Troy: The Story of the Iliad*
Taylor, Mildred D. *Roll of Thunder, Hear My Cry*
Twain, Mark. *The Adventures of Tom Sawyer*
Yep, Laurence. *Dragonwings*

DRAMA

Fletcher, Louise. *Sorry, Wrong Number*
Goodrich, Frances, and Albert Hackett. *The Diary of Anne Frank: A Play*

POETRY

Carroll, Lewis. "Jabberwocky"
Dickinson, Emily. "The Railway Train"
Frost, Robert. "The Road Not Taken"
Giovanni, Nikki. "A Poem for My Librarian, Mrs. Long"
Hughes, Langston. "I, Too, Sing America"
Longfellow, Henry Wadsworth. "Paul Revere's Ride"
Navajo tradition. "Twelfth Song of Thunder"

Neruda, Pablo. "The Book of Questions"
Sandburg, Carl. "Chicago"
Soto, Gary. "Oranges"
Whitman, Walt. "O Captain, My Captain"
Yeats, William Butler. "The Song of Wandering Aengus"

INFORMATIONAL TEXTS: ENGLISH LANGUAGE

Adams, John. "Letter on Thomas Jefferson"
Churchill, Winston. "Blood, Toil, Tears and Sweat: Address to Parliament on May 13th, 1940"
Douglass, Frederick. *Narrative of the Life of Frederick Douglass an American Slave, Written by Himself*
Petry, Ann. *Harriet Tubman: Conductor on the Underground Railroad*
Steinbeck, John. *Travels with Charley: In Search of America*

INFORMATIONAL TEXTS: HISTORY/SOCIAL STUDIES

Freedman, Russell. *Freedom Walkers: The Story of the Montgomery Bus Boycott*
Greenberg, Jan, and Sandra Jordan. *Vincent Van Gogh: Portrait of an Artist*
Isaacson, Phillip. *A Short Walk through the Pyramids and through the World of Art*
Lord, Walter. *A Night to Remember*
Monk, Linda R. *Words We Live By: Your Annotated Guide to the Constitution*
Murphy, Jim. *The Great Fire*
Partridge, Elizabeth. *This Land Was Made for You and Me: The Life and Songs of Woody Guthrie*
United States Preamble and First Amendment to the United States Constitution (1787, 1791)

INFORMATIONAL TEXTS: SCIENCE, MATHEMATICS, AND TECHNICAL SUBJECTS

California Invasive Plant Council. *Invasive Plant Inventory*
"Elementary Particles." *New Book of Popular Science*
Enzensberger, Hans Magnus. *The Number Devil: A Mathematical Adventure*
"Geology." *U*X*L Encyclopedia of Science*
Katz, John. *Geeks: How Two Lost Boys Rode the Internet Out of Idaho*
Macaulay, David. *Cathedral: The Story of Its Construction*

Mackay, Donald. *The Building of Manhattan*

Peterson, Ivars, and Nancy Henderson. *Math Trek: Adventures in the Math Zone*

Petroski, Henry. "The Evolution of the Grocery Bag"

"Space Probe." *Astronomy and Space: From the Big Bang to the Big Crunch*

NOTE

A complete list of text standards, exemplars, and resource materials as identified by the National Governors Association Center for Best Practices can be found at http://corestandards.org/ELA-Literacy.

FOUR

Grade 7 Strategies and Activities for Reading Literature

Choose literary text from Grades 6–8 text exemplars selections or other grade-level appropriate selections. Grades 6–8 text exemplars are noted with an (EX). Other appropriate grade-level selections with different publication dates include, but are not limited to, the following:

REALISTIC FICTION

A Corner of the Universe by Ann Martin (2004)
A Tree Grows in Brooklyn by Betty Smith (2006)
Anything But Typical by Nora Raleigh Baskin (2010)
Black Pearl by Scott O'Dell (2010)
Boost by Kathryn Mackel (2010)
Crazy Lady by Jane Leslie Conly (1995)
Crossover by Jeff Rud (2008)
Drama by Raina Telgemeier (2012)
Eight Cousins by Louisa May Alcott (2013)
Extreme Edge by Heather Kellerhals-Stewart (2007)
Journey of the Sparrows by Fran Leeper Buss (2002)
Kissing Doorknobs by Terry Spencer Hesser (1999)
My Life in Pink and Green by Lisa Greenwald (2010)
Night Hoops by Carl Deuker (2009)
Nothing But the Truth, A Documentary Novel by Avi (2010)
River Thunder by Will Hobbs (1999)
Sea Wolf by Jack London (1999)
Shabanu, Daughter of the Wind by Suzanne Fisher Staples (2012)
Son of the Mob (and sequels) by Gordon Korman (2004)

Swallowing Stones by Joyce McDonald (2012)
Taken by Norah McClintock (2009)
The Cay by Theodore Taylor (2003)
The Girl Who Threw Butterflies by Mick Cochrane (2010)
The Homecoming by Cynthia Voigt (2012)
The Maze by Will Hobbs (1999)
The Outsiders by S. E. Hinton (2006)
The Twenty-one Balloons by William Pene du Bois (2005)
The Yearling by Marjorie Kinnan Rawlings (2001)
Travel Team by Mike Lupica (2005)
Where the Lilies Bloom by Vera Cleaver and Bill Cleaver (2001)
Where the Red Fern Grows by Wilson Rawls (1996)
White Fang by Jack London (2013)

HISTORICAL FICTION

Beyond the Burning Time by Kathryn Lasky (1996)
Bug Boy by Eric Luper (2009)
Chains by Laurie Halse Anderson (2010)
Dragon's Gate by Laurence Yep (2001)
Call it Courage by Armstrong Speery (2008)
Fever, 1793 by Laurie Halse Anderson (2002)
Forge by Laurie Halse Anderson (2010)
Iron Thunder by Avi (2009)
Keeping the Castle by Patrice Kindl (2013)
Kidnapped by Robert Louis Stevenson (1982)
Little Women by Louisa May Alcott (1983)
Mary, Bloody Mary by Carolyn Meyer (2001)
My Antonia by Willa Cather (1994)
Out of the Dust by Karen Hesse (2009)
Sophia's War by Avi (2013)
The Bread Winner by Deborah Ellis (1990)
The Red Badge of Courage by Stephen Crane (1990)
Torn Thread by Anne Isaacs (2002)
Treasure Island by Robert Louis Stevenson (1993)
When I Crossed No-Bob by Margaret McMullan (2009)
Witch Child by Celia Rees (2009)

MYSTERY AND SUSPENSE

Change-up by John Feinstein (2010)
Dead Is the New Black by Marlene Perez (2008)
Double Identity by Margaret Peterson Haddix (2007)
Enola Holmes Mysteries by Nancy Springer (2007–2009)

Fake ID (and sequels) by Walter Sorrells (2005)
H.I.V.E. by Mark Walden (2008)
Hold Fast by Blue Balliett (2013)
Liar and Spy by Rebecca Stead (2013)
Red Kayak by Priscilla Cummings (2006)
Scat by Carl Hiassen (2012)
Seer of Shadows by Avi (2009)
Splendors and Glooms by Laura Amy Schlitz (2012)
Stormbreaker (a graphic novel) by Antony Horowitz (2006)
Tangerine by Edward Bloor (2006)
The Compound by S. A. Bodeen (2008)
The Intruders by E. E. Richardson (2009)
The London Eye Mystery by Sioban Dowd (2009)
The Rivalry: Mystery at the Army-Navy Game by John Feinstein (2010)
The Shade by K. L. Denman (2008)
The Trap by John Smelcer (2007)
The Man Who Was Poe by Avi (1997)
The Presence by Eve Bunting (2003)
When You Reach Me by Rebecca Stead (2010)

FANTASY AND SCIENCE FICTION

Anya's Ghost by Vera Brosgol (2011)
Doomsday by John Peel (1999)
Dr. Franklin's Island by Ann Halam (2003)
Everlost (and sequels) by Neal Shusterman (2009)
Full Tilt by Neal Shusterman (2009)
Gregor the Overlander by Suzanne Collins (2004)
Heir Apparent by Vivian Vande Velde (2004)
Inkheart (and sequels) by Cornelia Caroline Funke (2005)
Redwall by Brian Jacques (2002)
Runaway King by Jennifer A. Nielsen (2013)
The Boy Who Couldn't Die by William Sleator (2005)
The Chronicles of Narnia by C. S. Lewis (2001)
The City of Embers (and sequels) by Jeanne DuPrau (2004)
The Fellowship of the Ring by J. R. R. Tolkien (2012)
The Girl Who Borrowed Wings by Rinsai Rossetti (2012)
The Graveyard Book by Neil Gaiman (2010)
The Hero's Guide to Storming the Castle by Christopher Healy (2013)
The Hobbit by J. R. R. Tolkien (1989)
The Lightening Thief (and sequels) by Rick Riordan (2006)
The One and Only Ivan by Katherine Applegate (2012)
The Other Side of the Island by Allegra Goodman (2009)
The Princess Bride by William Goldman (2013)

The Return of the King by J. R. R. Tolkien (2001)
The Thief Lord by Cornelia Caroline Funke (2010)
The Time Machine by H. G. Wells (2013)
The Wind in the Willows by Kenneth Grahame (2012)
Things Not Seen by Andrew Clements (2006)
Tunnels (and sequels) by Roderick Gordon (2009)
Z for Zachariah by Robert C. O'Brien (2007)

POETRY

A Fire in My Hands by Gary Soto (2013)
Acolytes: Poems by Nikki Giovanni (2007)
Classic Poems for Girls (audio CD) by Lewis Carroll, Edward Lear, Robert Louis Stevenson, and Christina Rosetti (2012)
Edgar Allan Poe's Stories and Tales (cassette) by Edgar Allan Poe and full cast (2000)
In Their Own Voices: A Century of Recorded Poetry (audio CD) by Erica Jong, Al Young, and Rebekah Presson (1997)
Pablo Neruda: Poet of the People by Monica Brown (2011)
Poetry for Young People: Carl Sandburg by Frances Schoonmaker Bolin (2008)
Poetry for Young People: Edgar Allan Poe by Brod Bagert (2008)
Poetry for Young People: Emily Dickinson by Frances Schoonmaker Bolin (2008)
Poetry for Young People: Henry Wadsworth Longfellow by Frances Schoonmaker Bolin (2008)
Poetry for Young People: Langston Hughes by David Roessel (2013)
Poetry for Young People: Lewis Carroll by Edward Mendelson (2008)
Poetry for Young People: Maya Angelou edited by Dr. Edwin Graves Wilson (2013)
Poetry for Young People: Robert Frost by Gary Schmidt (2008)
Poetry for Young People: Robert Louis Stevenson by Frances Schoonmaker Bolin (2008)
Poetry for Young People: Walt Whitman by Jonathan Levin (2008)
Poetry for Young People: William Butler Yeats by Jonathan Allison (2002)
Poetry for Young People: William Shakespeare edited by David Scott Kastan (2008)
The Children's Homer (audio CD) by Padraic Colum and Robert Whitfield (2000)

SUGGESTED ACTIVITIES

- Compare and Contrast—In class discussions on how to cite a source, create an example of APA, Chicago, MLA, or other formats your teacher wants you to use. Create a citation for a one-author and two-author text, a magazine article (print and online), newspaper article (print and online), TV and radio transcript, video documentary, online encyclopedias and databases, and websites for a class wall chart and/or yourself. Your teacher may give you other suggestions. Discuss how each is similar and different. Keep the examples for future reference. (RL.7.1, SL.7.1)

- Take Notes—Use sticky notes in your texts to identify textual evidence and inferences and refer to the notes in class or group discussions. (RL.7.1, SL.7.1)
- Take Notes—Create a variation of the two-column notes when citing evidence. On the left side of your notes, label the column "Explicit Details/Examples" and on the right side, label the column "Inferred Details/Examples." As you take notes, write your evidence in the appropriate column and include page numbers for future discussion. (RL.7.1)
- Take Notes—Use a T-chart or concept web to take notes when preparing arguments. When using a T-chart, write the argument point on one side and supportive evidence and citation on the other. If using a concept web, write the argument point inside the concept circle and the supporting evidence and citation on the outside of the circle, attached to the circle. (RL.7.1)
- Take Notes—Use a "It Says-I Say-And So" three-column graphic organizer. Label the first column "It Says," label the second column "I Say," and label the third column "And So." Read a given selection. In the first column, write down words, phrases, ideas, or images from the reading the material. Jot down the page or paragraph numbers, too, for easy reference. Also write down the main ideas. In the second column, write what you already know about the topic and similar experiences you have had in the same situation. Think about what you read and what you know and make an educated guess about what you read. (RL.7.1)
    - Use literature familiar to students to teach the process.
- Nonlinguistic Representations—Create posters, dioramas, collages, or murals to illustrate specific and inferred details in the text, adding the page number(s) to the illustrations. Be prepared to share your evidence in small group or class discussion. (RL.7.1, SL.7.1)
- Cooperative Learning—In small groups play interactive online games to learn how to create citations in APA or MLA. Go to http://depts.washington.edu/trio/quest/citation/apa_mla_citation_game/indes.htm. (RL.7.1)
- Make Predictions—Look at the title of your selection. Based solely on the title and cover art if any, make a prediction about what will happen in the story. As you get to the middle of the selection, make

additional predictions. Cite page numbers to support your thinking. Continue to the end and check your predictions. Be ready to state any personal experiences that led you to your predictions. Was your prediction correct? What are the similarities and differences in what you experienced and what happened in the text? Discuss the similarities and differences in group or class discussions. (RL.7.1, SL.7.1)
- Hypothesize and Test—Cite several pieces of textual evidence to support analysis when working to generate and test hypotheses. (RL.7.1)
- Questions—Use stem questions in appendix C to help students cite textual evidence. (RL.7.1)
    - Use questions such as: What might you infer from . . . and where did you see that?
    - Explain and cite which clues or details from the text helped you to infer . . .
    - What is implied by the sentence . . . and how would you cite the inference?
    - Which statement from the selection explains . . . and how would you cite the statement?
    - Which sentence is evidence that . . . and how would you cite it?
- Questions—When you think about citing a source, what questions do you need to answer? (RL.7.1)
    - What format am I to use?
    - What information from the text do I need?
    - Are there specific page numbers I need?
    - Where is an accurate and reliable place to look on the internet if I have a question on a citation?
- Homework and Practice—Use various games and activities from the book *Plagiarism! Plagiarism! 25 Fun Games and Activities to Teach Documenting and Sourcing Skills to Students* by Kathleen Fox (2010). (RL.7.1)
- Homework and Practice—Practice citations by going on a citation hunt. Go to the website www.education.com/activity/article/Citation_Hunt_middle. (RL.7.1)
- Homework and Practice—Search texts for information and cite references in appropriate formats. See www.brighthubeducation.com/middle-school-english-lessons/11380-scavenger-hunt-to-learn-about-referencing-and-citations. (RL.7.1)
- Compare and Contrast—Compare and contrast the theme or central idea in a piece of literature and how they are developed through the course of the text. Create a timeline or flowchart to

illustrate how either the theme or central idea is developed giving specific instances from the text. Include page numbers for each detail listed so you can refer to it in discussion. Select three stories or poems with similar themes or central ideas and show the similarities and differences in how the theme or central idea is developed using a graphic organizer. You may share your organizer in group or class discussion (RL.7.2, RL.7.1, SL.7.1)
- Compare and Contrast—Select two or three stories from the exemplars or other grade-appropriate selections and create a two- or three-circle Venn diagram to compare and contrast the settings, events, and themes in the texts. You may share your diagrams with the group or class. (RL.7.2, SL.7.1)
- Summarize—Write a brief objective summary for each resource you are going to use in research, including the citation for the source. Add page numbers as you use the resource. The summary will help you as you write to remember the information from each source. (RL.7.2, RL.7.1)
- Summarize—Select two texts with similar themes or central ideas. Complete a narrative frame to summarize each text. Create a T-chart to compare and contrast the two texts. Share your chart with a partner, group, or the class. (RL.7.2, SL.7.1)
- Summarize—Use the title of the book or story or poem and create an acrostic summary. (RL.7.2, W.7.10)
- Summarize—Do a quick write (a thirty- to sixty-second draft) to summarize what you have learned or have done with regard to a topic. (RL.7.2)
- Summarize—Complete a SQRRR (Survey/Question/Read/Recite/Review) summary frame on your current reading assignment. (RL.7.2, RL.7.4, RL.7.10)
- Summarize—Create a plot diagram to summarize a text. (RL.7.2)
- Summarize—Use the Somebody-Wanted-But-So-Then summary frame to summarize the text. (RL.7.2)
- Summarize—Create mnemonics to help remember key details of people or events. (RL.7.2)
- Take Notes—As you read, take notes to describe the theme or central idea and how it is developed over the course of the text. Mark your text with several sticky notes to cite explicit textual and inferred evidence of the development of the theme or central idea. In small or large group or class discussion, discuss how it is applicable to your lives today. (RL.7.2, RL.7.1, SL.7.1)
- Take Notes—Create a journal or a spreadsheet (paper or electronic) for fiction to identify the title, author, theme, or central idea of the text, points of view, setting, characters, and key character behaviors. Highlight inferred details. Indicate page numbers that help you determine the information. (RL.7.2, RL.7.1)

- Nonlinguistic Representation—Create a comic strip to illustrate the theme of or to summarize a selection. (RL.7.2)
- Nonlinguistic Representation—Create a rap or song based on your notes and summaries of events. Present your rap or song to the class. (RL.7.2, SL.7.1, SL.7.6)
- Nonlinguistic Representation—Role-play or pantomime key scenes to convey the theme or central idea of a selection and how it is developed through the text. (RL.7.2, SL.7.6)
- Nonlinguistic Representation—Create concept webs or illustrated timelines to summarize selections. (RL.7.2)
- Nonlinguistic Representation—Select a graphic novel or other appropriate selection and create an illustrated book jacket to summarize the text. (RL.7.2)
- Nonlinguistic Representation—Create book jackets or bookmarks for stories, poems, and drama to illustrate the theme or central idea. The illustrations or drawings should be representative of particular details. (RL.7.2)
- Cooperative Learning—As you read, conduct a Kagan Cooperative Learning structure called Paraphrase Passport[1] to create objective summaries of a larger text selection. Students collaborate in groups of four. The first student begins to summarize the story or selection. The next student must paraphrase what the first student said and then contribute more to the summary. The process continues until all have had a chance to listen and to speak. Groups should alternate positions so the same student is not always first or last. (RL.7.2, SL.7.1)
- Cooperative Learning—Use the Kagan Cooperative Learning structure of Think-Pair-Share.[2] After reading a selection, students get into pairs and each thinks about the theme or central idea. You may also write your thoughts out as you think about the theme or central idea. One partner then shares their theme or central idea, citing textual and inferred evidence, while the other partner listens; then partners switch roles and repeat the process. (RL.7.2, SL.7.1)
  - Use Think-Pair-Share to share the day's reading or library book assignment or to reflect on large chunks of information during class lecture.
- Predictions—On file cards or small note cards write words that are relevant to the story you are discussing in class. You will need fifteen words for each pair of students; students are to place cards on their desk with words down. Ask students to create a T-chart on paper, labeling the left side "Words" and the right side "Predictions." Students then turn over five cards and write the words on the left side of their chart. Pairs silently think about the words for one minute in terms of theme or central idea. Pairs converse and

make a prediction based on the words, writing the prediction on the right side of the paper. Repeat the process two more times, until all words have been revealed and three predictions have been made. Predictions may be changed as the new words appear. Let students share their predictions with the class. Read the selection to determine the theme or central idea. (RL.7.2, SL.7.1)
- Questions—Use stem questions from appendix C to help determine or discuss the central idea or theme of a text and how it is developed throughout the text. (RL.7.2)
    - Use questions such as
        - Which sentence supports the central idea or theme of a selection?
        - Which details from the text contribute to the development of the theme or central idea?
        - What examples can you find to illustrate the development of the theme or central idea over the course of the text?
        - What techniques are used by the author to develop the theme or central idea?
        - What do characters say and do?
        - How does the plot itself or individual events help to reveal the theme?
        - Are minor characters important to the development and if so, how?
        - How well did the author use illustrations, print, chapter titles, and other text features to help develop the theme or central idea through the text?
- Homework and Practice—Write a paragraph to describe how the theme or central idea is developed throughout a text, citing page numbers to support your analysis. Which details helped you determine the theme or central idea? You may share your ideas in group or class discussion. (RL.7.2, RL.7.1, W.7.10)
- Homework and Practice—Practice writing objective summaries for various texts. (RL.7.2, W.7.10)
- Homework and Practice—Before reading a graphic novel, look at the illustrations. Can you infer the theme? Cite several pieces of textual evidence to support your inference. Then read the text to check your inferences. (RL.7.2, RL.7.1)

> *Amazing Greek Myths of Wonder and Blunders* by Michael Townsend (2010)
> *Diary of a Wimpy Kid: The Third Wheel* by Jeff Kinney (2012)
> *Dragonbreath #7* by Ursula Vernon (2012)
> *Dr. Jekyll and Mr. Hyde* by John K. Snyder III (2009)

Ghost Circles: Bone by Jeff Smith (2008)
Hardy Boys #7: The Opposite Number by Scott Lodbell (2013)
Nancy Drew: The Charmed Bracelet by Stephan Petrucha (2006)
Stormbreaker: The Graphic Novel by Antony Johnston (2006)
The Graveyard Book by Neil Gaiman (2010)
The Invention of Hugo Cabret by Brian Selznick (2007)
The Lightening Thief: The Graphic Novel by Rick Riordan (2010)
The Stonekeeper by Kazu Kibuishi (2008)

- Compare and Contrast—Create a graphic organizer (concept web, double-T chart, etc.) to detail how the setting was used in two stories considering the components of time, place and the social customs, dress and manners of the characters. As you read, cite evidence from the text to support your analysis. Do the setting details simply describe where the action takes place, or does where it take place affect the events? Use your notes to write an informative essay to compare and contrast the role of settings in two similar stories you select. Use a variety of sentence structures, appropriate capitalization, punctuation and spelling, precise and concise language, and figurative language where appropriate. Edit for grammar and mechanics. (RL.7.3, RL.7.1, W.7.2, L.7.1b–c, L.7.2, L.7.3)
- Compare and Contrast—Create and complete problem-solution frames for stories or drama as you read. Compare selections with similar problems and contrast the solutions using a T-chart or Venn diagram to show how characters responded or changed. Jot down page numbers to cite your evidence in support of your analysis. (RL.7.3, RL.7.1)
- Compare and Contrast—Create a multicolumn chart to describe multiple characters in the same text (no more than five). You will need a column for each character and a row for each of the following: physical description, what the character says, what others say about the character, what the character does. Make note of the page numbers beside each detail or inference. Use the information to write a comparison and contrast essay to show how the characteristics of the characters affect the plot. Use a variety of sentence structures, appropriate capitalization, punctuation and spelling, precise and concise language, and figurative language where appropriate. Edit for grammar and mechanics. (RL.7.3, RL.7.1, W.7.2, L.7.1b–c, L.7.2, L.7.3)
- Take Notes—Create a timeline. As you read, note various settings on the top of the line with either text or a simple illustration. Below the line indicate how each setting affected the characters or the plot. (RL.7.3, RL.7.1, SL.7.1)
- Take Notes—Create a T-chart. On the left side jot down the characters names from your story or drama. On the right, write down any

decisions made by each character because of the setting or how the character was affected by the setting. (RL.7.3)
- Take Notes—State the mood of the selection and three examples to support your opinion. Share your examples with a partner and discuss how the mood affected what happened in the story or drama. (RL.7.3, SL.7.1)
- Take Notes—Create a T-Chart. On the left, write down language, illustrations, and layout. On the right, give specific examples of each, including page numbers that help convey the mood in a story or drama. Share your chart with a partner and discuss how all the elements work together to convey the mood. (RL.7.3, SL.7.1)
- Nonlinguistic Representation—Identify the key episodes in a story, drama or poem. Create a wall mural for each key episode. Read aloud or role play the episodes in front of the mural. Discuss as a class the impact of the setting image on the episodes. (RL.7.3, SL.7.6)
- Hypothesize and Discuss—Think about the setting of a story. As a group or a class, work together to answer this question: How is the setting significant to character development or plot resolution? Create an if/then statement and discuss. For example: *If* the setting of a story is significant to the story, *then* the setting is significant in character development. Or: *If* the setting of a story is significant to the story, *then* the setting is significant to the plot resolution. Share your responses as a class. (RL.7.3, SL.7.1)
- Hypothesize and Test—What happens if the setting is changed in a realistic fiction text? Can the events still happen? Why or why not? Rewrite a story or tell a story, changing key details of the setting to test your hypothesis. Use a variety of sentence structures, appropriate capitalization, punctuation and spelling, precise and concise language, and figurative language where appropriate. Edit for grammar and mechanics. (RL.7.3, W.7.3)
- Hypothesize and Test—What happens if the setting is changed in a historical fiction text? Can the events still happen? Why or why not? Rewrite a story or tell a story, changing key details of the setting to test your hypothesis. Use a variety of sentence structures, appropriate capitalization, punctuation and spelling, precise and concise language, and figurative language where appropriate. Edit for grammar and mechanics. (RL.7.3, W.7.3)
- Hypothesize and Test—If a historical event is changed, how are the people affected? Rewrite a story or tell a story, changing key details of the event to test your hypothesis. Use a variety of sentence structures, appropriate capitalization, punctuation and spelling, precise and concise language, and figurative language where appropriate. Edit for grammar and mechanics. (RL.7.3, W.7.3)

- Homework and Practice—Create a list of plot events, setting details, and character traits for each major character in a story or drama. Create a three-circle Venn diagram and label the circles "Plot," "Setting," and "Character Traits." Transfer the items from your list and write them in the appropriate place on your Venn diagram with regard to what that item affected. You could have a specific event that had an effect on the plot, was affected by the setting, and caused specific character traits so all three items would be in the center of the Venn. You might have some items that are only plot, setting, or character traits and some that might belong in two sections. Ultimately, students need to see how several elements interact together in a story or drama. (RL.7.3, SL.7.1)
    - Compare and contrast your Venn to those of other students. Where are the differences and why would there be differences?
- Homework and Practice—Analyze how the playwright Louise Fletcher uses particular elements of drama such as setting and dialogue to create dramatic tension in her play *Sorry, Wrong Number.* Create a chart to cite examples of each and note page numbers for easy reference in class discussion. (RL.7.3, SL.7.1)
- Homework and Practice—Consider the following elements of a story: dialogue, descriptive language, structure, symbolism, humor, irony, suspense, strong verbs, and text divisions. Create a concept web to show how these elements interact with each other in a story or drama. Attach specific examples from the text to each part of the web and add page numbers to the examples for quick reference. (RL.7.3)
- Homework and Practice—Consider the following elements of a drama: theme, plot, mood, characters, dialogue, music, and visual elements. Create a concept web to show how these elements interact with each other in a story or drama. Attach specific examples from the text to each part of the web and add page numbers to the examples for quick reference. (RL.7.3)
- Compare and Contrast—Choose two fictional texts on similar topics, one that is rich with figurative language and/or connotative meanings and another that contains neither. Write an essay to compare and contrast the two selections. Use a variety of sentence structures, appropriate capitalization, punctuation and spelling, precise and concise language, and figurative language where appropriate. Edit for grammar and mechanics. Cite specific evidence to support your analysis. Which is the more appealing of the two selections? (RL.7.4, RL.7.1, W.7.2)
- Compare and Contrast—Choose two poems: one with rhyme and/or alliteration; one without. Compare and contrast the impact of the

poem with rhyme and/or alliteration to the one without in an essay. Which sounds better to the ear? Which do you prefer? Why do you think the authors chose to write with or without rhyme and alliteration? How does the rhyme and alliteration affect specific verses or stanzas? Does the lack of rhyme and alliteration affect the poem? Use a variety of sentence structures, appropriate capitalization, punctuation and spelling, precise and concise language, and figurative language where appropriate. Edit for grammar and mechanics. (RL.7.4, W.7.2)

- Poetry books with alliteration and rhyme—

    A Little Bit of Nonsense by Denise Rogers (n.d.)
    Great Lakes Rhythm and Rhyme by Denise Rogers (2001)
    Swimming Upstream: Middle School Poems by Kristine O'Connell George (2002)
    Tongue Twisters for Kids by Riley Weber (2013)
    Tongue Twisters by Riley Weber (2013)

- Take Notes—Create a class word wall and add and sort words and phrases in context as you learn them. Include examples of figurative language. (RL.7.4)
    - Words can also be added to individual vocabulary files or an electronic dictionary. Define what the author implies or says if different from the "real" definition.
    - Review vocabulary words from time to time to study the various meanings. Also note whether words or phrases are regional or historical dialects or are derived from other languages.

- Take Notes—Create a card file with index cards. As you come to a new word, write the word on a card, along with the definition as it is used in the sentence; note any affixes and their meanings as well as the word derivation. Also note whether the word is an example of regional or historical dialect. (RL.7.4)
    - Sort words throughout the year by affixes, roots, or derivations.
    - Add definitions to words or phrases as they are used in different context.
    - Add figurative language words and phrases as you see them in text.

- Take Notes—Create a class dictionary. As you learn new words and phrases throughout the year, ask a volunteer to write the new word in the class dictionary. Use a three-ring binder with loose-leaf paper and alphabetical tabs so you can add to it throughout the year. Define the word or phrase as it is used in context. You may also create an electronic form of it as well using Word or another program. Students may look up the words or phrases as needed. Include poetry terms and definitions as well. (RL.7.4)

- Take Notes—Use an Alphabox to organize and define new words and phrases for each new story, poem, or unit. You may wish to create an electronic form in Excel so the size of the boxes can easily be adjusted to fit terms and definitions. (RL.7.4)
- Nonlinguistic Representation—Read a variety of poetry. Choose a favorite poem with alliteration. On poster board and in the center, write the letter from your poem that is repeated. Write it large enough that it stands out. Around the letter write all the words from the poem that have that letter repeated. On the back of your poster write a paragraph to describe the impact of the repetition on the stanza or poem. Share your poster with your class. (RL.7.4, SL.7.1)
    - You can do the same for rhyme. Write all words that have the same rhyme in your poem on a poster. On the back of your poster write a paragraph to describe the impact of the rhyme on the stanza or poem. Share your poster with your class.
- Nonlinguistic Representation—Read aloud or memorize and recite a poem. Create a simple movement for each one or two repeated words or sounds or rhymes. After all students have read or recited, discuss the impact of the repetitions or rhymes on you as you read or recited out loud. (RL7.4, SL.7.1)
    - You might try these:
        "Betty Botter" by Mother Goose
        Fox in Socks by Dr. Seuss (1965)
        The Butter Battle Book by Dr. Seuss (1984)
        "The Raven" by Edgar Allen Poe
        "Three Grey Geese" by Mother Goose
- Cooperative Learning—Students get into pairs. Each student will select five words from the word wall, card file, or maybe a class dictionary. Write down the words. Do a Kagan Cooperative Learning structure called Think-Pair-Share[3] as both think about their words and the feelings they get from the words. Then one at a time, share the words, their definitions, and the connotative meaning. (RL.7.4, SL.7.1)
- Questions—Use stem questions to ask about meanings of unknown words and phrases. (RL.7.4)
    - What is the meaning of the word as it is used in context?
    - What are other meanings of the word?

- What part of speech is the word?
- Using context clues, how would you define...
- What clues helped you to define the word or phrase....
- What is the root of the word?
- Does the word have affixes?

- Homework and Practice—Practice reviewing word meanings and connotations using crossword puzzles. Create your own crossword puzzles and share with the class. There are several puzzle makers on the Internet or you can use graph paper and create your own. (RL.7.4)

    www.puzzle-maker.com
    www.discoveryeducation.com/free-puzzlemake
    http://edhelper.com/crossword_free.htm
    http://worksheets.theteacherscorner.net/make-your-own/crossword

- Homework and Practice—Practice defining words using a definition frame and print or digital resources. (RL.7.4, SL.7.1)
    - Create flashcards with terms and definitions; work in pairs to quiz each other.
- Homework and Practice—Write a simple poem of your own with alliteration and rhyme. Share your poem with a partner. Discuss your word choices and why. Are there other words that might have been a better choice? Make constructive suggestions to help your partner where possible. How does your word choice impact your poem? (RL.7.4, SL.7.1)
- Homework and Practice—Choose a poem the class is going to read. Enlarge the copy so you can cut up individual lines, giving one line to each student. Ask students to think about their line as to the meaning of the words, including figurative and connotative meanings. Ask students to read their line, give meaning to unknown words or phrases, and state the word or phrase that impacts the meaning or tone of the line and how. (RL.7.4, SL.7.1)
- Homework and Practice—Identify examples of figurative and descriptive language in various texts. Share examples with the class. Discuss in class any connotative meanings and how figurative and descriptive language impacts stories or dramas. (RL.7.4, SL.7.1)
- Homework and Practice—Look at current advertisements in print and on TV. Identify examples of rhyme and alliteration. Students should bring examples in to class and as a class, discuss the impact of the figurative language, connotative meanings, and use of alliteration and rhyme in the ads. How is the consumer affected by the ad? (RL.7.4, SL.7.1)

- Homework and Practice—Create an advertisement slogan for your favorite product. Find a picture of your favorite product, cut it out and attach it to poster paper, and write your slogan across the top of the page. Share your slogans with the class. Did you purposely use a specific word or letter for repetition or rhyme? (RL.7.4, SL.7.1)
- Homework and Practice—As a class read the poem "The Siege of Belgrade" by Alaric Alexander Watts aloud. Notice how the author used every letter of the alphabet in order to begin each line and set up the alliteration. Does the poem still make sense? Choose a topic as a class and write a poem like the one you read. The poem should tell a story or explain an event. Each student can write one line or small groups can write several lines. After the poem is written, read it aloud as a class or divide the class into small groups to read assigned sections. Do certain lines have more impact than others? Why? (RL.7.4, W.7.10, SL.7.1)
- Homework and Practice—Rewrite a stanza or short poem changing words to eliminate repetition or rhyme. Read the poem first and then read the rewrite. Share and discuss your poems or stanzas with the class. Which poems have the most impact? (RL.7.4, SL.7.1)
- Compare and Contrast—Compare and contrast in an informative essay format the form or structure of Gary Soto's poem "Oranges" to Soto's *Novio Boy: A Play*. Create a graphic organizer to identify the similarities and differences and use the information to write the essay to answer the following question: How does the form or structure contribute to the meaning? Use a variety of sentence structures, appropriate capitalization, punctuation and spelling, precise and concise language, and figurative language where appropriate. Edit for grammar and mechanics. (RL.7.5, W.7.2, W.7.7, L.7.1b–c, L.7.2, L.7.3, L.7.5)
- Compare and Contrast—Compare and contrast English sonnets, Italian sonnets, and Spenserian sonnets. Create a three-circle Venn diagram to show the similarities and differences in their forms. Research to identify examples of each and add the titles to the diagram. (RL.7.5)
- Take Notes—As you read drama or poetry, take notes as to the text structure and how the structure contributes to the meaning. (RL.7.5)
- Nonlinguistic Representation—Illustrate the meaning of a sonnet or soliloquy on a poster or mural. Write the title and author on the illustration as well. Share the illustration and the meaning with the class. (RL.7.5, SL.7.6)
    - All students could illustrate the same sonnet or soliloquy and could then compare and contrast the illustrations with regard to how students interpreted the meaning.

- Cooperative Learning—Divide the class into small groups of three to four students. Create a list of specific text structures that can be found in texts in the classroom or in selections that you give to students. Give students a list of the structures to find and conduct a text structure treasure hunt. Students should cite the example of the structure and continue until all groups have found all structures on their list. Share the cited treasure with the class and discuss how each is a good example. (RL.7.5, SL.7.1, RL.7.1)
- Predictions—Scan titles, subtitles, headings, or other text features in drama or poetry. Skim the text to identify the text structure. Based on what you see, write down your prediction as to the possible meaning of the text based on the text features and structure. Share your prediction with a partner. Read the text to see if you are correct. Share your prediction and findings with the group or class. (RL.7.5, SL.7.1)
- Hypothesize and Test—What would happen if you rewrote a sonnet or a passage from a drama in a different form or used a different structure? Does the text form or structure still contribute to the meaning? Write a hypothesis and test it. Share your hypothesis and results with the class. (RL.7.5, W.7.3)
- Questions—Use stem questions in appendix C to ask about the structural elements of dramas and the form of poetry and how they contribute to meaning. (RL.7.5)

    - What are the similarities and differences in the structural elements of . . . ?
    - How does the sentence, chapter, scene, or stanza fit into the overall structure of the text?
    - How well does _____ contribute to the meaning?
    - Describe the relationship between the scene or stanza and the meaning.
    - What might you infer from the structure or form of a text?

- Homework and Practice—Describe how the form or structure of a drama or poem contributes to the meaning. Read aloud or memorize and recite a soliloquy or monologue to the class. Share with the class the form or structure of the reading and how it contributed to the meaning. Cite several pieces of textual or inferred evidence to support your analysis. (RL.7.5, RL.7.1, SL.7.6)

    Acting Scenes and Monologues for Kids: Original Scenes and Monologues Combined into One Very Special Book! by Bo Kane (2010)
    Daisies and Raindrops Sonnets for Children by Scott Ennis (2011)
    Just Me: 100 Monologues for Teens by Phyllis C. Johnson (2013)
    Magnificent Monologues for Kids: 2 by Chambers Stevens (2008)
    Suppertime Sonnets by Kate Sherrod (2011)

William Shakespeare: Poetry for Young People by David Scott Kasten, Marina Kasten, William Shakespeare, Glenn Harrington (2000)

- Homework and Practice—Read a selection of drama or poetry and notice how it is organized and the text structure used. Is it description, sequence, compare and contrast, cause and effect or problem/solution? In paragraph form, state the structure used and identify three to five examples of the structure. Cite your textual evidence. Share your findings with a partner, small group or class. What did the structure help you learn from the text? (RL.7.5, SL.7.1)
- Homework and Practice—Rewrite a passage or stanza from drama or poetry. Read the revision into the original. Discuss in small or large groups if and how the meaning is changed because of your revision. (RL.7.5, SL.7.1)
- Homework and Practice—Practice selecting a passage, stanza, or scene and journaling about how it contributes to the meaning. Share your thoughts with a partner. Cite several pieces of specific details from the text. (RL.7.5, RL.7.1, SL.7.1)
- Homework and Practice—Write a critique about the text as a whole, evaluating how well the text, illustrations and other features work together to contribute to the meaning. What could the author have done to make the meaning better or clearer? Use a variety of sentence structures, appropriate capitalization, punctuation and spelling, precise and concise language, and figurative language where appropriate. Edit for grammar and mechanics. Follow the format given to you. (RL.7.5, W.7.2, L.7.1b–c, L.7.2, L.7.3)
- Homework and Practice—Write a position paper to support your analysis of how the overall structure or form of a text contributes to the meaning. Use a variety of sentence structures, appropriate capitalization, punctuation and spelling, precise and concise language, and figurative language where appropriate. Edit for grammar and mechanics. (RL.7.5, W.7.1, W.7.7, L.7.1b–c, L.7.2, L.7.3, L.7.5)
- Compare and Contrast—Choose a selection from the Grades 6–8 text exemplars or other grade-appropriate texts. Create one character map for each of two characters from the same text by folding a piece of paper into four equal sections. Write one character's name at the top of the page. In one square, state what other characters think about your character. In the rest of the squares, state how you feel about your character, what your character says and does, what your character looks like, and what she feels. Repeat for the second character. Jot down page numbers in each square that helped you with the information for that square. Mark inferred information with a highlighter. Use a variety of sentence structures, appropriate capitalization, punctuation and spelling, precise and concise lan-

guage, and figurative language where appropriate. Edit writing for grammar and mechanics. (RL.7.6, RL.7.1, W.7.2, W.7.10, SL.7.1, L.7.1b–c, L.7.2, L.7.3)

- Use the character maps for group or class discussion about what the text says explicitly or infers, or to explain how the author develops the narrator's or speaker's point of view.
- Use the character maps to write a comparison and contrast essay that describes the points of view of two or more characters.
- Change up your character maps from time to time to include the actions/reactions of others to the character, personality traits, strengths/weaknesses, and attitudes of the characters toward each other.

- Compare and Contrast—Create a three-circle Venn diagram or other appropriate graphic organizer and chart the points of view of the main characters. Write an essay using the information to compare and contrast either multiple points of view in the same story or multiple points of view on the same topic from different stories. You may be asked to share your information in small or large group discussions. Use a variety of sentence structures, appropriate capitalization, punctuation and spelling, precise and concise language, and figurative language where appropriate. Edit your writing for grammar and mechanics. Cite several pieces of textual evidence to support your analysis. (RL.7.6, RL.7.1, W.7.2, SL.7.1, L.7.1b–c, L.7.2, L.7.3)
- Compare and Contrast—Who is the narrator or speaker in a story? Is the narrator's or speaker's point of view different from other characters? If so, how does the author develop the different point of view? How does the author develop other points of view? Compare and contrast in essay format the point of view of the narrator or speaker and the point of view of one other character. Cite several pieces of textual evidence. Use a variety of sentence structures, appropriate capitalization, punctuation and spelling, precise and concise language, and figurative language where appropriate. Edit your writing for grammar and mechanics. (RL.7.6, RL.7.1, W.7.2, L.7.1b–c, L.7.2, L.7.3)
- Compare and Contrast—Determine the point of view of three main characters. Create a three-circle Venn diagram to illustrate the similarities and differences in the points of view of the characters. Discuss as a class. (RL.7.6, SL.7.1)
- Summarize—Summarize the point of view of the main character using a Somebody-Wanted-But-So-Then summary frame. (RL.7.6)
- Take Notes—Identify the narrator or speaker and one other character in your text. Illustrate how the author developed the point of

view of both characters using a T-chart. Think about the actions, decisions, and descriptions of each to help you determine the points of view. Cite several pieces of textual evidence to support your analysis. (RL.7.6, RL.7.1)
- Take Notes—Create a multicolumn chart or concept web to illustrate the author's point of view of the narrator or speaker and other characters. Use headings such as Characters, Physical Description, What Characters Say, What Characters Think, What Characters Do, What Others Say and Think about Them, and Author's Point of View. Fill in all columns of the chart or web, except the last column, with examples from the text as you read. When you have finished the story and the chart or web, get with a partner or in small or large group discussions and use the information to determine the author's point of view of each character. (RL.7.6, SL.7.1)
- Hypothesize and Test—What would happen if an author created all characters and the narrator or speaker with the same point of view? Write a hypothesis and test it by rewriting sections to reflect the same points of view. Use a variety of sentence structures, appropriate capitalization, punctuation and spelling, precise and concise language, and figurative language where appropriate. Edit for grammar and mechanics. Share your revisions with the group or class. Does the story change and if so, how? (RL.7.6, W.7.3, SL.7.1)
- Predictions—Read or look at the title, chapter titles (if there are any), textual features, illustrations and any blurbs about the author for a selection you are reading. Predict the point(s) of view the author will develop prior to reading based on the titles, illustrations, and blurbs. (RL.7.6)
- Questions—Use stem questions to ask about the points of view of the narrator/speaker and the other characters. (RL.7.6)
    - Who is the narrator or speaker and how do you know?
    - What is the narrator's or speaker's point of view?
    - How does the author develop the narrator's or speaker's point of view?
    - How does the author contrast the various points of view?
    - Why does the author say _____ when he or she really means _____?
    - What are the other points of view presented in the story?
- Homework and Practice—Demonstrate how the author developed the narrator's/speaker's or characters' points of view by presenting key sections of your text to the class. Let others try to determine the point of view based on your presentation of the events. (RL.7.6, SL.7.6)
- Homework and Practice—Create a class chart to list the various genres of literature, writing the genres down the side of the chart.

Across the top of the chart, make headings for "Titles" and "Author Development." As you read, beside the appropriate genre, fill in the chart by writing the title of the texts read and list how the author developed and contrasted points of view. When several are on the chart, discuss as a class any relationships you see between the genre and how the author developed or contrasted the points of view. (RL.7.6, SL.7.6)

- Compare and Contrast—In small groups, conduct research to determine techniques unique to audio, film, stage, or multimedia productions. Create a graphic organizer to illustrate the techniques for each. As a class, discuss how each is similar and different and give examples of each medium that incorporates the identified techniques. (RL.7.7, SL.7.1)

  - Read a story or excerpt. Listen to the audio version. Listen again as you follow along with the text. Use sticky notes to indicate places that are different and how the story was affected by the use of audio techniques. If you choose to watch a filmed, staged, or multimedia version, take notes as to how the story was affected by the various techniques used for each medium. Use the information from your research and your listening and/or viewing experience to individually write an informative essay to compare and contrast a written story, drama, or poem to its audio, filmed, staged, or multimedia version, analyzing the effects of techniques unique to two different mediums. Do you have a better understanding of the story? Use a variety of sentence structures, appropriate capitalization, punctuation and spelling, precise and concise language, and figurative language where appropriate. Edit your writing for grammar and mechanics. (RL.7.6, W.7.2, W.7.7, L.7.1b–c, L.7.2, L.7.3)
  - Check for stage productions in your area or YouTube for other versions. You can also choose from these:

    A Tree Grows in Brooklyn by Betty Smith (2008)
    A Tree Grows in Brooklyn by Betty Smith (Caedmon Audiobook, 2008)
    A Wrinkle in Time by Madeleine L'Engle (2007) (EX)
    A Wrinkle in Time: The Graphic Novel by Madeleine L'Engle and Hope Larson (2012) (EX)
    A Wrinkle in Time by Madeleine L'Engle (Echo Home Bridge Entertainment, 2011) (EX)
    A Wrinkle in Time by Madeleine L'Engle (Listening Library Audio CD, 2012) (EX)
    Black Ships before Troy: The Story of the Iliad by Rosemary Sutcliff (2005) (EX)

Black Ships before Troy: The Story of the Iliad (AudioGO, 2011) (EX)
Call of the Wild by Jack London (2013)
Call of the Wild by Jack London (Mission Audiobook, 2012)
Dragonwings by Laurence Yep (2001) (EX)
Dragonwings by Laurence Yep (Harper Festival Audio CD, 2007) (EX)
Jabberwocky and Other Poems (Dover Thrift Editions) by Lewis Carroll (2001) (EX)
Poetry Speaks to Children (book and CD) edited by Elise Paschen (2005)
Little Women by Louisa May Alcott (2013) (EX)
Little Women by Louisa May Alcott (Sony Pictures Home Entertainment, 1994) (EX)
Little Women by Louisa May Alcott (Listening Library Audio CD, 2011) (EX)
"O Captain! My Captain" by Walt Whitman (EX)
"O Captain! My Captain" by Walt Whitman (Epic Audio Collection) (EX)
Roll of Thunder, Hear My Cry by Mildred Taylor (2004) (EX)
Roll of Thunder, Hear My Cry by Mildred Taylor (Listening Library Audio CD, 2005) (EX)
The Adventures of Tom Sawyer by Mark Twain (1998 or others) (EX)
The Adventures of Tom Sawyer by Mark Twain (Blackstone Audio Classic Collection, 2008) (EX)
The Adventures of Tom Sawyer by Mark Twain (Platinum Disc Studio, 2012) (EX)
The Dark Is Rising by Susan Cooper (1999) (EX)
The Dark Is Rising by Susan Cooper (Listening Library Audio CD, 2007) (EX)
The People Could Fly by Virginia Hamilton (1993) (EX)
The People Could Fly by Virginia Hamilton (Audible Audio, 2005) (EX)
"The Railway Train" by Emily Dickinson
"The Railway Train" by Emily Dickinson (Epic Audio Collection)
The Road Not Taken and Other Poems by Robert Frost (Dover Thrift Edition, 1993)
"The Road Not Taken" by Robert Frost (audio download at www.learnoutloud.com)
"The Song of Wandering Aengus" by William Butler Yates
"The Song of Wandering Aengus" by William Butler Yates (Epic Audio)

- Take Notes—As you read, listen to and/or view a story, drama, or poem, take notes as to any techniques you notice used in the various medium. Create a graphic organizer to incorporate all mediums and note techniques used. Use the graphic organizer in future discussions or writing assignments. (RL.7.7)
- Nonlinguistic Representations—Look through magazines, brochures, or the Internet to locate a variety of graphics (captions, diagrams, pictures, illustrations). Create a class wall chart of techniques used in various mediums. Try to locate examples of each technique. Cut out or print the examples and attach to the chart with a description of the technique used and how it is being used in the illustration. Discuss each example as a class. (RL.7.7, SL.7.1)
- Cooperative Learning—In small groups, choose a favorite short story, children's story, or poem. Pretend you are going to create an audio, filmed, staged, or multimedia version of the written text. What would you do and how would you do it? Refer to the charts and information you have about the techniques used in the different mediums and write out your plan to create a new version. Each group will make an audio version to be presented to the class incorporating a variety of audio techniques. Then choose one other medium and rewrite the text so that the various techniques for that medium can be seen. You will need to assign speaking parts, scripts, stage directions, sound, costumes, and camera and lighting directions to name a few. Before each presentation, all students should have access to the print version and should read it silently to themselves. Groups then present the audio versions to the class, while students follow along on the written copy. As a class, compare and contrast the written versions to the audio versions with regard to the techniques used and how they contribute to the meaning. Groups will then present their story in the other chosen medium, describing what they would do and how. (RL.7.7, SL.7.1, SL.7.6)
- Compare and Contrast—Compare and contrast in essay format a fictional portrayal of a time, place, or character and a historical account of the same period as a means of understanding how authors of fiction use or alter history. Compare and contrast the texts with regard to characters, events, actions, and circumstances and describe how the author used or altered history to fit the plot in a fictional portrayal. Do research to identify key people and key events from the historical period. Write your information on a graphic organizer. Then read one of the texts, noting same or similar characters and events as well as different characters or events on another graphic organizer. Read the next text and do the same. Write your essay based on the information on your graphic organizers. Cite several pieces of textual evidence to support your anal-

ysis. Use a variety of sentence structures, appropriate capitalization, punctuation and spelling, precise and concise language, and figurative language where appropriate. Edit for grammar and mechanics. (RL.7.9, RL.7.1, W.7.2, L.7.1b–c, L.7.2, L.7.3)

- Select topics such as

    Middle Ages
    Salem Witch Trials
    Revolutionary War
    Civil War
    Holocaust
    Great Depression

- Compare and Contrast—Compare and contrast a fictional character to one from a historical account of the same period. Create a two-circle Venn diagram to show how the characters are alike and different with regard to events that happened to them and around them, character traits, and how they responded to situations. Use the information to write a comparison and contrast essay. How did the author use or alter history for the fictional character? Use a variety of sentence structures, appropriate capitalization, punctuation and spelling, precise and concise language, and figurative language where appropriate. Edit your essay for grammar and mechanics. (RL.7.9, W.7.2, L.7.1b–c, L.7.2, L.7.3)
- Compare and Contrast—Compare and contrast Laurence Yep's fictional portrayal of Chinese immigrants in *Dragonwings* to historical accounts of the same period in order to get a better understanding of how the author used or altered history. Write an essay and use a variety of sentence structures, appropriate capitalization, punctuation and spelling, precise and concise language, and figurative language where appropriate. Edit your essay for grammar and mechanics. (RL.7.9, W.7.2, L.7.1b–c, L.7.2, L.7.3)
- Take Notes—As you read, take notes in two-column format. On one side note and cite details from the fictional text and on the other side note and cite details from the historical account. (RL.7.9, RL.7.1)
- Questions—As you conduct research to compare and contrast fictional and historical accounts, consider the following questions: (RL.7.9)
    - What is the period of the text?
    - Where did the characters/historical person live?
    - What did each do?
    - What problems were encountered and how did each overcome the problems?

- What major events occurred? Which events did the author alter?
- Does the author's style make the characters more or less believable?
- How else did the author alter or use history?

- Take Notes—As you read, take notes about how your characters are affected by the time period in which they live. (RL.7.10)
- Questions—As you read, consider and discuss responses to the following questions in small or large group situations. (RL.7.10, SL.7.1)

  - What is the genre?
  - How does the genre affect the characters? Events? Settings?
  - What is the overall theme?
  - When and where does the story take place? Is the story related to a historical event?

- Questions—Throughout the year you will read a variety of literature. To help determine books of interest, interview a book by "asking questions" about the book. (RL.7.10)

  - Look at the title and cover art if any. Does the title sound interesting?
  - Look at the author's name. Have you read any other books by the author?
  - What do you know about the author?
  - Read the blurb inside the book or on the back of the book. Does it sound interesting or similar to others you have read on the same topic?
  - What is the genre of the book? Is it a genre you generally like to read? If you don't know the genre, are there any key works to help you determine the genre such as "mystery" or "biography"?
  - Look at the cover. Are there any seals designating the book as an award-winning book?

    Coretta Scott King Award
    Michael L. Printz Award
    National Book Award
    Newbery Award
    Young Adult Library Services Award

    - Is the text too difficult or too easy to read?

- Homework and Practice—Read and comprehend literature in the Grades 6–8 text complexity band proficiently. (RL.7.10, SL.7.1, SL.7.6)

- Practice reading every night, self-correcting when you make mistakes.
- Stop frequently when reading and restate in your own words what you have read.
- As you read, make mental predictions about what will happen next and check to see if you were correct.
- Record stories or poems for others to hear.
- Create skits or plays based on literary text.
- Play music in the background related to theme and topics.
- Dress in costume as you read—keep it simple—wear hats, scarves, vests; something symbolic of the topic or theme.
- Role-play the main character in stories, drama, or poems.
- Memorize and present favorite passages or poems.

  Read All About It! Great Read-Aloud Stories, Poems and Newspaper Pieces for Pre-Teens and Teens by Jim Trelease (1993)

  Reading Comprehension, Grades 7–8 by Instructional Fair (2003)

  Swimming Upstream: Middle School Poems by Kristine O'Connell George (2002)

- Homework and Practice—Vary the genres of texts you read throughout the year. Create a class chart of recommended reading. Add text titles and authors to the chart, including those read as a class and others read through independent reading. Set a goal to read two to three books from each genre in addition to those read as a class. (RL.7.10)
- Homework and Practice—To help students better visualize characters, individuals, events, and settings, incorporate a variety of visuals and experiences (RL.7.10)

  - Attend plays in your area.
  - Post calendar pictures, book jackets, magazines, or other printed pictures around the room that represent your current topics and refer to them when taking notes.
  - Look for original prints you could borrow from libraries or parents.
  - Create areas in the room representative of settings or events.
  - Create artifact tables—find pictures or symbolic replicas of items that represent people, characters, or events.
  - Eat a meal that would be symbolic of your theme or topic.
  - Listen to music that represents your topic during free time or played softly in the background while taking notes.

- Homework and Practice—Read aloud or listen to various grade level texts. (RL.7.10)

NOTES

1. Kagan, S., & Kagan, M. (1997). *Kagan Cooperative Learning Smart Card* (pp. 2–3). San Clemente, CA: Kagan Publishing.
2. See Kagan, S., & Kagan, M. (1997) for further information.
3. See Kagan, S., & Kagan, M. (1997) for further information.

FIVE

Grade 7 Strategies and Activities for Reading Informational Text

Choose informational text from Grades 6–8 text exemplars or other appropriate grade-level selections. Grades 6–8 text exemplars are noted with an (EX). Other appropriate grade-level selections include, but are not limited to, the following:

AUTOBIOGRAPHIES

Boy: Tales of Childhood by Roald Dahl (1993)
Chuck Close: Face Book by Chuck Close (2012)
Gifted Hands: The Ben Carson Story by Ben Carson (1996)
Grace, Gold and Glory: My Leap of Faith by Gabby Douglas (2012)
Knots in My Yo-Yo String: The Autobiography of a Kid by Jerry Spinelli (1998)
Knucklehead: Tall Tales and Mostly True Stories of Growing Up Scieszka by Jon Scieszka (2008)
Maria Tallchief: America's Prima Ballerina by Larry Kaplan and Maria Tallchief (2005)
Running a Thousand Miles for Freedom by William Craft and Ellen Craft (1999)
The Story of My Boyhood and Youth: An Autobiography by John Muir (2010)
The Privilege of Youth: A Teenager's Story by Dave Pelzer (2004)
Within Reach: My Everest Story by Mark Pfetzer (2000)

BIOGRAPHIES

Anne Frank Beyond the Diary: A Photographic Remembrance of Holocaust Years by Rudd Van der Rol (1995)
B. Franklin, Printer by David A. Adler (2001)
Bone Detective: The Story of Forensic Anthropologist Diane France by Lorraine Jean Hopping (2006)
Diary of a Young Girl by Anne Frank (1993)
Good Brother, Bad Brother: The Story of Edwin Booth and John Wilkes Booth by James Giblin (2005)
J. K. Rowling: Extraordinary Author by Victoria Peterson-Hilleque (2010)
Joan of Arc: The Lily Maid by Margaret Hodges (1999)
Steve Jobs: The Man Who Thought Different by Karen Blumenthal (2012)
The Defenders by Ann McGovern (1987)
The Forbidden Schoolhouse: The True and Dramatic Story of Prudence Crandell and Her Students by Suzanne Jurmaine (2005)
The Great and Only Barnum: The Tremendous, Stupendous Life of Showman P. T. Barnum by Candace Fleming (2009)
The Magic Never Ends: The Life and Works of C. S. Lewis by John Ryan Duncan (2001)
The Trouble Begins at 8: A Life of Mark Twain in the Wild, Wild West by Sid Fleischman (2008)
The Upstairs Room by Johanna Reiss (1990)
The Wright Brothers: How They Invented the Airplane by Russell Freedman (1994)

MEMOIRS

A Few Seconds of Radiant Filmstrip: A Memoir of Seventh Grade by Kevin Brockmeier (2014)
A Friend Called Anne: One Girl's Story of War, Peace and a Unique Friendship with Anne Frank by Jacqueline van Maarsen (2005)
Children of Willesden Lane: Beyond the Kindertransport—A Memoir of Music, Love and Survival by Mona Golabek (2003)
Chinese Cinderella by Adeline Yen Mah (2010)
Four Perfect Pebbles: A Holocaust Story by Lila Perl (1999)
Guts by Gary Paulsen (2002)
Night by Elie Wiesel (2006)
No Pretty Pictures: A Child of War by Anita Lobel (2008)
Red Scarf Girl: A Memoir of the Cultural Revolution by Ji-Li Jiang (2008)
Restless Spirit: The Life and Work of Dorothea Lange by Elizabeth Partridge (1998)
Rutka's Notebook by Rutka Laskier (2008)

Sky: A True Story of Resistance during World War II by Hanneke Ippisch (1996)

Surviving the Angel of Death: The True Story of a Mengele Twin in Auschwitz by Eva Mozes Kor (2012)

GENERAL NONFICTION

An Indian Winter by Russell Freedman (1992)

Candy Bomber: The Story of the Berlin Airlift's "Chocolate Pilot" by Michael O. Tunnell (2010)

Growing Up in Coal Country by Susan Campbell Bartoletti (1999)

Hitler Youth: Growing Up in Hitler's Shadow by Susan Bartoletti (2005)

If Stones Could Speak by Marc Aronson (2010)

Left for Dead: A Young Man's Search for Justice for the USS Indianapolis by Peter Nelson (2003)

Moonbird: A Year on the Wind with the Great Survivor B 95 by Phillip Hoose (2012)

Photo by Brady: A Picture of the Civil War by Jennifer Armstrong (2005)

September 11, 2001: Attack on New York City by Wilborn Hampton (2003)

Smile by Raina Teigemeier (2010)

Team Moon by Catherine Thimmesh (2006)

The Great Fire by Jim Murphy (2010)

The Kid Who Invented the Popsicle by Don Wulffson (1999)

The Voice That Challenged a Nation: Marian Anderson and the Struggle for Equal Rights by Russell Freedman (2011)

SUGGESTED ACTIVITIES

- Compare and Contrast—In class discussions on how to cite a source, create an example of APA, Chicago, MLA, or another format your teacher wants you to use. Create a citation for a one-author and two-author text, a magazine article (print and online), newspaper article (print and online), TV and radio transcript, video documentary, online encyclopedias and databases, and websites for a class wall chart and/or yourself. Your teacher may give you other suggestions. Discuss how each is similar and different. Keep the examples for future reference. (RI.7.1, SL.7.1)
- Take Notes—Use sticky notes in your texts to identify textual evidence and inferences and refer to the notes in class or group discussions. (RI.7.1, SL.7.1)
- Take Notes—Create a variation of the two-column notes when citing evidence. On the left side of your notes, label the column "Explicit Details/Examples" and on the right side, label the column

"Inferred Details/Examples." As you take notes, write your responses in the appropriate column and include page numbers for future discussion. (RI.7.1)
- Take Notes—Use a T-chart or concept web to take notes when preparing arguments. When using a T-chart, write the argument point on one side and supportive evidence and citation on the other. If using a concept web, write the argument point inside the concept circle and the supporting evidence and citation on the outside of the circle, attached to the circle. (RI.7.1)
- Take Notes—Use a "It Says-I Say-And So" three-column graphic organizer. Label the first column "It Says"; label the second column "I Say"; and label the third column "And So." Read a given selection. In the first column, write down words, phrases, ideas, or images from the reading the material. Jot down the page or paragraph numbers, too, for easy reference. Also write down the main ideas. In the second column, write what you already know about the topic and similar experiences you have had in the same situation. Think about what you read and what you know and make an educated guess about what you read. (RI.7.1)
  - Use informational text familiar to students to teach the process.
- Nonlinguistic Representations—Create posters, dioramas, collages, or murals to illustrate specific and inferred details in the text, adding the page number(s) to the illustrations. Be prepared to share your evidence in small group or class discussion. (RI.7.1, SL.7.1)
- Cooperative Learning—In small groups play interactive online games to learn how to create citations in APA or MLA. Go to http://depts.washington.edu/trio/quest/citation/apa_mla_citation_game/indes.htm. (RI.7.1)
- Make Predictions—Look at the title of your selection. Based solely on the title and cover art if any, make a prediction about what will happen in the text. Flip through the rest of the pages, looking at illustrations, captions, graphics, etc., and make additional predictions. Cite page numbers to support your thinking. Read the text and check your predictions. Be ready to state any personal experiences or previous knowledge that led you to your predictions. Was your prediction correct? What are the similarities and differences in what you experienced or knew about and what happened in the text? Discuss the similarities and differences in group or class discussions. (RI.7.1, SL.7.1)
- Hypothesize and Test—Cite several pieces of textual evidence to support analysis when working to generate and test hypotheses. (RI.7.1)

- Questions—Use stem questions in appendix C to help students cite textual evidence. (RI.7.1)
  - Use questions such as: What might you infer from . . . and where did you see that?
  - Explain and cite which clues or details from the text helped you to infer . . .
  - What is implied by the sentence . . . and how would you cite the inference?
  - Which statement from the selection explains . . . and how would you cite the statement?
  - Which sentence is evidence that . . . and how would you cite it?
- Questions—When you think about citing a source, what questions do you need to answer? (RI.7.1)
  - What format am I to use?
  - What information from the text do I need?
  - Are there specific page numbers I need?
  - Where is an accurate and reliable place to look on the Internet if I have a question on a citation?
- Cooperative Learning—In small groups play interactive online games to learn how to create citations in APA or MLA. Go to hhttp://depts.washington.edu/trio/quest/citation/apa_mla_citation_game/indes.htm. (RI.7.1)
- Homework and Practice—Use various games and activities from the book *Plagiarism! Plagiarism! 25 Fun Games and Activities to Teach Documenting and Sourcing Skills to Students* by Kathleen Fox (2010). (RI.7.1)
- Homework and Practice—Practice citations by going on a citation hunt. Go to the website www.education.com/activity/article/Citation_Hunt_middle. (RI.7.1)
- Homework and Practice—Search texts for information and cite references in appropriate formats; www.brighthubeducation.com/middle-school-english-lessons/11380-scavenger-hunt-to-learn-about-referencing-and-citations. (RI.7.1)
- Summarize—Read selected passages to determine two or more central ideas of a text and describe how it is developed through the text; then write an objective summary of the text. (RI.7.2)
  - You might use: *Non-fiction Reading Comprehension Grades 7–8* by Schyrlet Cameron and Suzanne Myers (2012)
- Summarize—Create acrostic summaries using the title of the text. Share summaries in small groups or with the class. (RI.7.2, SL.7.1)

- Summarize—Create concept webs, Somebody-Wanted-But-So-Then frames, problem-solution frames, and narrative frames to create objective summaries of the text. (RI.7.2)
- Summarize—Write a bio-poem to summarize information about a person you have studied. (RI.7.2, W.7.10)
- Take Notes—Use a two-column note format. As you read, jot down on the left side what you think the central ideas of a text are and on the right, jot down several pieces of textual evidence to support what the text says and your inferences in support of your analysis. (RI.7.2, RI.7.1)
- Take Notes—Create outlines to illustrate main ideas and specific details to help determine the central ideas of a text. (RI.7.2)
- Take Notes—Read a variety of texts with content applicable to today's seventh grade student such as self-esteem, academic pressures, bullying or other antisocial behaviors, or disappointment and rejection. As you read, take notes on the key points. Then in your journal, write how you can apply the information to your life today. You may also be asked to participate in class discussions on the issues. (RI.7.2, W.7.10, SL.7.1)

   Help! I'm in Middle School . . . How Will I Survive? by Merry Gumm (2005)
   Middle School: How I Survived Bullies, Broccoli, and Snake Hill by James Patterson (2013)
   Middle School: The Worst Years of My Life by James Patterson (2012)
   The Complete Idiot's Guide to Surviving Peer Pressure for Teens by Hilary Cherniss (2001)
   The Drama Years: Real Girls Talk about Surviving Middle School . . . Bullies, Brands, Body Image and More by Haley Kilpatrick and Whitney Joiner (2012)
   Teen Ink: Our Voices, Our Visions by John and Stephanie Meyer (2000)

    - Create a timeline for each text to illustrate the central ideas of each and how they are developed over the course of the text.
    - Decide which book is most helpful in your opinion to boys or to girls in terms of information presented. Write a position paper to defend your opinion. (W.7.1, L.7.1b–c, L.7.2, L.7.3)
    - Create a book jacket with an objective summary on the back for each book.

- Nonlinguistic Representation—Create a graphic organizer to illustrate the central ideas and supporting details for each idea. You

may be asked to share your organizer with a partner, small group or the class. (RI.7.2, SL.7.1)
- Nonlinguistic Representation—Create a double timeline. On the top at the beginning of the line, state one main idea. On the bottom of the line, state another main idea. Plot the development of each idea by writing an event or a detail that furthers the central idea on either the top or bottom of the line as they happened relative to each other. (RI.7.2)
- Cooperative Learning—As you are reading to determine the central idea, stop frequently to do a Kagan Cooperative Learning structure called Think-Pair-Share.[1] When given the signal, think about the information you have just read, jotting notes or drawing pictures or symbols to help you remember particular details. Then pair up and take turns sharing your thoughts and information. (RI.7.2)
- Questions—In class or group discussions, consider the following questions: (RI.7.2)
    - What are the central ideas of the text?
    - What does the author use to develop the central ideas?
    - How well does the author develop the central ideas throughout the text?
    - Are there underlying themes in the text? If so, what are they and how do you know?
    - Is the theme applicable to your life today?
- Homework and Practice—Choose your favorite nonfiction text and evaluate how well the author developed the central ideas over the course of the text. Make note of several examples of textual evidence to support your claim. Present your evaluation to the group or class. (RI.7.2, RI.7.1, SL.7.1)
- Homework and Practice—Create a mnemonic to help you remember the central ideas and main details of a large selection of text or to create a summary. (RI.7.2)
- Take Notes—Create a flowchart when taking notes to illustrate how ideas influenced individuals or events or how individuals influenced ideas or events. (RI.7.3)
- Take Notes—Create a double timeline to show interactions. List events on the top of the line and place reactions or influences that occurred as a result of the event on the bottom of the timeline directly below the event. Cite several pieces of textual evidence to support your analysis. (RI.7.3, RI.7.1)
- Take Notes—Create character maps for the main and supporting people in informational texts. Your map should include what each thought and felt, decisions each made because of thoughts or feelings, actions each took, and how others reacted to each because of their thoughts, feelings, or actions. (RI.7.3)

- For subjects of biographies, memoirs or autobiographies, include accomplishments, overreactions, underreactions, and how the person responded to events or ideas.
- Take Notes—Add new words or phrases and their meanings to your word wall or vocabulary card file or notebook as they are used in context. Add new meanings to existing words or phrases as well. Designate words or phrases using a symbol or color to reflect regional or historical dialects as well as languages other than English. (RI.7.4)
  - In class discussion of text, describe the impact of specific words on meaning and tone of the text. (SL.7.1)
- Take Notes—Complete a definition frame for words and phrases that have special historical significance. (RI.7.4)
- Take Notes—To help solidify a new word or phrase, write the term or phrase on an index card. Draw a picture or symbol that represents the word or phrase. Write down one example of the word or phrase. Write a hint to help you remember the definition (such as a mnemonic). Write a sentence using the word or phrase similar to the way it was used in the text. Share your pictures, examples, and sentences with the class. (RI.7.4, SL.7.1)
- Take Notes—Create crossword puzzles or word searches based on terms and/or definitions. (RI.7.4)
- Nonlinguistic Representation—Create illustrated definitions. Fold a sheet of paper so that you have four squares. Write the term in the center of the page. In top left square, define the term in your own words and draw a picture or image of what the word symbolizes to you. In the top right square, write three facts you know about the term and add a picture or image of each fact. In the bottom left, state what the term is *not* like. In the bottom right, state what the term *is* like. Compare definitions as a class. (RI.7.4, SL.7.1)
- Nonlinguistic Representation—Create a class mural or poster to define important terms as they are used in texts. Write the term in the center of the poster and draw illustrations or symbols of what the term means. (RI.7.4, SL.7.1)
- Nonlinguistic Representation—For key words in a new unit, create a class mural or poster with words written on it in no particular order. Draw arrows or lines to indicate which words are connected/related to other words. Circle any words that are not connected. Discuss the relationship of the words to each other. (RI.7.4, SL.7.1)
- Questions—As you discuss vocabulary, consider the following questions in your discussions: (RI.7.4)
  - Is the word a simile or metaphor or other example of figurative language?

- What is the connotation of the word or phrase?
- What is the impact of the word or phrase on the meaning and tone?
- Are there other words or phrases that would help deepen the meaning? If so, what?
- How are the terms related to each other?
- What is the relationship of the term(s) to the topic?
- Are there Greek or Latin affixes?
- What clues from the text helped to define the word or phrase?

- Take Notes—Nonfiction text structure refers to how the writer organizes and develops ideas. The most important text structures are description or list, sequence or time order, compare and contrast, cause and effect, and problem/solution (http://comsewogue.org/webpages/drosenquist/reading_workshop.cfm?subpage=640939).
As you read make note of the structure(s) used to organize the selection and describe how the major sections contributed to the whole text and development of ideas. Be prepared to share your thoughts in class discussion. Note and cite signal words to help you determine the organizational structure used. (RI.7.5, RI.7.1, SL.7.1)
- Nonlinguistic Representation—Create a banner to represent the major sections of a text and how each contributes to the development of ideas. Write the title and author at the top of the banner and divide the banner into the different sections represented by the organizational structure. Share with a partner or the class and discuss how each section contributes to the whole of the text. (RI.7.5, SL.7.1)
- Nonlinguistic Representation—Create a concept web to illustrate the structure(s) used in a text. The web should include examples and key words from the text. Cite several pieces of textual evidence to support your analysis. (RI.7.5)
- Nonlinguistic Representation—Create a scrapbook representative of the major sections of an informational text you read and organize it in a way that represents the structure used in your text. Each page should contain images or pictures with descriptions that enable the reader to see the development of the central ideas over the course of the text. Share your scrapbook with the class. Be sure to include the title and author on the cover of your scrapbook. (RL.7.5, SL.7.1)
- Predictions—Perform a SQ (Survey-Question) on your reading assignments. Based on section titles, headings, subheadings, illustrations/photographs, make predictions about what you will read and how the text is organized. Then complete the RRR (Read-Recite-Review) and track your predictions as you read. (RI.7.5)

- Hypothesize and Test—How would your comprehension of the material be affected if authors did not use an organizational structure? Write and test your hypothesis. (RI.7.5)
- Hypothesize and Test—Can your text be written in a different organizational structure? Write your hypothesis and test it by writing out what you would change and how you would change it. Identify key words to signal the organization and write sentences with the key words to reflect the content of the text. Share your hypothesis and plan with the class. (RI.7.5, SL.7.1, SL.7.6)
  - "Test" the hypothesis as a class in class discussion.
- Questions—Consider the following questions in discussions about an author's use of text structure and the structures used. (RI.7.5)
  - Does the author use a combination of structures? Is so, which ones and why?
  - Does the combination make the meaning more clear, or is it confusing and why? Give examples and cite your pieces of evidence.
  - How well do the print, text features, and layout contribute to the development of the ideas?
  - Why do authors use different structures for different genres?
  - Would this text have worked better in another structure?
  - What are the similarities and differences in the structural elements of . . . ?
  - What are the major sections of the text?
  - Cause and Effect Questions—
    - What happened?
    - Why did it happen?
    - What caused it to happen?
    - What was the effect? What were the results? Outcomes?
    - How did prior events cause or influence the main event?
  - Compare and Contrast Questions—
    - What is being compared? In what way?
    - What characteristics do they have in common?
    - How are they different?
  - Description Questions—
    - What person, place, thing, event, or concept is being described?
    - If it is a thing, how does it work? What does it do?
    - How would you classify the topic?
    - What are the most common characteristics?

- What is important to remember about it?
- Problem and Solution—
    - What is the problem? Who has a problem?
    - What is causing the problem?
    - Why is it a problem?
    - What has been tried so far as a solution?
    - What are possible solutions?
    - What are the pros and cons of each possible solution?
    - What can be done to prevent the problem again in the future?
- Sequence Questions—
    - What items, steps, or events are listed?
    - What are the major events that occur?
    - Do they have to happen in this order?
    - What would happen if the order changed?
    - What are the steps, directions, or procedures to be followed?
    - What is the final outcome?

- Homework and Practice—Choose your favorite informational text. Write a position paper to defend or oppose an author's choice of the organizational structure used and how well the major sections contribute to the text as a whole and to the development of ideas. Use a variety of sentence structures, appropriate capitalization, punctuation and spelling, precise and concise language, and figurative language where appropriate. Edit for grammar and mechanics. Cite several pieces of evidence to support your analysis. (RI.7.5, RI.7.1, W.7.2, L.7.1b–c, L.7.2, L.7.3)
- Compare and Contrast—Read various articles from different sources about the same topic or idea. Choose two articles by different authors on the same topic. What is each author's purpose in writing the article or text? How do you know? What strong words are used that state an opinion or feeling? Write an essay to compare and contrast the purposes and points of view of the different authors and how they distinguish their position from that of others. Use a variety of sentence structures, appropriate capitalization, punctuation and spelling, precise and concise language, and figurative language where appropriate. Edit for grammar and mechanics. Cite several pieces of textual evidence to support analysis of what the text says explicitly and what it infers. You may be asked to share your essay with the class. (RI.7.6, RI.7.1, SL.7.1, L.7.1b–c, L.7.2, L.7.3)

- Compare and Contrast—Read two or three articles or informational texts by the same author. Create a concept web to illustrate the author's purpose and point of view for the texts. Include examples on the web and cite page numbers for your evidence. Discuss any similarities or differences in the author's purpose or points of view as a class or small group. (RI.7.6, RI.7.1, SL.7.1)
- Summarize—Write an objective summary of the author's point of view for various texts to illustrate any bias in a biography, noting specific examples of biased language. (RI.7.6, RI.7.1, W.7.10)
- Take Notes—As you read, make note of examples of bias or propaganda, citing the specific language used that reveals the bias or propaganda. Note page numbers of the examples. (RI.7.6, RI.7.1)
- Take Notes—Create a T-chart to identify specific language that reflects point of view or bias. On one side of the chart note the point of view or bias and on the other side, jot down examples from the text with page numbers to support your analysis. (RI.7.6, RI.7.1)
- Nonlinguistic Representation—Choose and read a biography. Note examples of bias and jot down the page numbers for quick reference. Create a book jacket for the text to illustrate the central ideas and the bias in the text. On the "inside" of the book jacket, write a five-paragraph critique in which you analyze the bias in the text. Does the bias show the subject of the biography in a good or bad way? How so? Does the bias work against the author? Use a variety of sentence structures, appropriate capitalization, punctuation and spelling, precise and concise language, and figurative language where appropriate. Edit for grammar and mechanics. Cite several pieces of evidence to support your analysis. (RI.7.6, RI.7.1, W.7.1, L.7.1b–c, L.7.2, L.7.3)
- Hypothesize and Test—Why would an author of a biography use biased language in the biography? Write and test a hypothesis for a biography you have read to determine the bias and the reason for the bias citing several pieces of explicit and inferred evidence to support your analysis. (RI.7.6, RI.7.1, W.7.10)
- Hypothesize and Test—Read the title, table of contents (if any), and blurbs on the inside or back of the book. Write a hypothesis about the author's purpose and/or point of view. Read to prove or disprove your hypothesis. Cite several examples from the text that prove or disprove your hypothesis. (RI.7.6, RI.7.1)
- Questions—Consider a variety of questions in group or class discussions when talking about the author's purpose and point of view. (RI.7.6)
    - Are there strong words that state opinions or feelings in the text?
    - What is the author's point of view?

- What key words or phrases help you to identify the point of view? Cite examples from text.
- Why might the author have this opinion or feeling?
- Is there background information that would help you to understand the author's point of view?
- Do others have the same point of view for the same reasons?
- What are you able to see from the author's point of view?
- How did the author support his point of view?
- Are there discrepancies in the support?
- Why did the author write the selection, i.e., to provide readers with information? To describe a person, event, or issue? To express their own thoughts and feelings? To persuade readers to think about an issue in a certain way and to take action? To entertain the reader? Cite evidence to support your thoughts.
- Based on the title or cover art (if any), what can you predict the selection will be about?
- Are you influenced by the author's point of view to take an action? If so, what action will you take?

• Homework and Practice—Gather and copy or create several paragraphs that represent an author's purpose to entertain, inform, persuade or describe. Cut out the paragraphs and laminate the paragraphs so they can be used again. Be sure to have enough for each student to read at least one paragraph. Put paragraphs in a basket and let students draw a paragraph from the basket. When all students have chosen, let students read their paragraph aloud while others listen for key words. Students then guess the purpose of the paragraph and cite evidence to support their choice. (RI.7.6, RI.7.1, SL.7.1)

• Homework and Practice—Some children's book authors and illustrators have video interviews available to watch online. Check readingrockets.org for more than one hundred interviews. You can also check out readersread.com, NPR.org, bellaonline.com, wiredforbooks.org, and missliterati.com. You might also locate contact information on the back or inside the cover of the book. Authors sometimes have websites as well. Please check out all sites prior to using in class. (RI.7.6, SL.7.1, SL.7.6)

- Read a book or two by a particular author. Contact the author for a possible teleconference with your class. Discuss with the author her purpose or point of view in a particular book. Share with the author what you learned from the text and how you can use her words in your life.

- Compare and Contrast—Read a selection first and write in your journal or discuss with a partner any opinions you formed about the main character. Then listen to an audio or watch a video version of the text. Did your opinion(s) change? Did you notice any instances of bias in any of the different mediums? Did your opinion change because of the medium's portrayal of the subject? How does the delivery affect the impact of the words? Create a two- or three-circle Venn diagram to organize your thoughts. Write an informative essay to compare and contrast your selections. Use a variety of sentence structures, appropriate capitalization, punctuation and spelling, precise and concise language, and figurative language where appropriate. Edit for grammar and mechanics. Cite several pieces of evidence to support your analysis. (RI.7.7, RI.7.1, W.7.1, SL.7.1, L.7.1b–c, L.7.2, L.7.3)
- Compare and Contrast—Choose a topic and prepare and present a two-to-three-minute speech for the class. Write the speech and your teacher will see that all students have a copy. Then record the speech. Finally, prepare a multimedia presentation where you present the speech to the class using visual aids as necessary. Students will read the text versions silently to themselves, listen to the audio versions as a class, and will then watch as you present your speech in person. Take notes as you read and listen, noting examples of propaganda or bias and how the medium affects the impact of the words. When all students have presented their speeches, students will choose one presentation to compare and contrast in an informative essay. Use a variety of sentence structures, appropriate capitalization, punctuation and spelling, precise and concise language, and figurative language where appropriate. Edit for grammar and mechanics. Cite several pieces of evidence to support your analysis. (RI.7.7, RI.7.1, W.7.1, SL.7.1, L.7.1b–c, L.7.2, L.7.3)
  - Use topics such as

    Pet peeves
    Best free-time activities
    Favorite celebrities
    Summer vacation spots
    Environmental issues in the community
    Fashions of our time
    The evolution of communication
    My hero
    Best cartoon hero
    Unsung heroes in our community
    Unsung heroes in our school
    Conversation is a lost art
    Importance of sportsmanship in athletics

- Compare and Contrast—Compare and contrast a text to an audio, video, or multimedia version of the text, analyzing each medium's portrayal of the subject. How does the delivery affect the impact of the words? Create a two- or three-circle Venn diagram to organize your thoughts. Write an informative essay and use a variety of sentence structures, appropriate capitalization, punctuation and spelling, precise and concise language, and figurative language where appropriate. Edit for grammar and mechanics. Cite several pieces of evidence to support your analysis. (RI.7.7, RI.7.1, W.7.1, L.7.1b–c, L.7.2, L.7.3)

    "Blood, Toil, Tears and Sweat: Address to Parliament on May 13th 1940" by Winston Churchill (EX)
  http://kids.learnoutloud.com/kids-catalog/History/speeches
    "I Have a Dream" by Dr. Martin Luther King Jr.
    "Gettysburg Address" by Abraham Lincoln
    "Give Me Liberty or Give Me Death" by Patrick Henry
    "First Inaugural Address" by President George Washington
    "Plymouth Oration" by Daniel Webster
  www.learnoutloud.com/free-audio-video/history/speeches
    "Speech on Women's Right to Vote" by Susan B. Anthony
  www.famous-speeches-and-speech-topics.info
    "On Surrender to US Army" by Chief Joseph of the Nez Perce
    "Dissolution of the Long Parliament" by Oliver Cromwell
    "Blood and Iron" by Otto Von Bismarck
    "Farewell to Baseball" by Lou Gehrig
  Anne Frank: The Diary of a Young Girl by Anne Frank and B. M. Mooyaart (1993)
  The Play of "The Diary of Anne Frank" (Heinemann Plays for 11–14) by Francis Goodrich and Albert Hackett (1995)
  The Diary of Anne Frank (Well Go USA DVD, 2009)
  Anne Frank: The Diary of a Young Girl: The Definitive Edition by Anne Frank (Listening Library Audio CD, 2010)
    "The Midnight Ride of Paul Revere" by Henry Wadsworth Longfellow (EX)
    "The Midnight Ride of Paul Revere" by Henry Wadsworth Longfellow (www.myaudioschool.com/?p=716) (EX)
    "The Midnight Ride of Paul Revere" by Henry Wadsworth Longfellow (www.reelyredd.com/0807paulrevere.htm) (EX)
  The Miracle Worker by William Gibson (1984)
  The Miracle Worker: A Play by William Gibson (2008)

The Miracle Worker by William Gibson (MGM Studio, 2001)

- Summarize—Write a summary of the speeches or presentations given in class in your journal. What key concept can you take from the speeches or presentations and apply to your daily life? (RI.7.7)
- Questions—Consider the following questions when comparing and contrasting a text to an audio, video or multimedia version of the text. (RI.7.7)
    - How did each medium portray the subject?
    - How did the delivery impact the words?
    - Did you notice stress in the voice when watching a video or listening to an audio version?
- Summarize—Write a summary to trace the arguments and specific claims supported by sound reasons and relevant and sufficient evidence in text or presentations. (RI.7.8, RI.7.1, W.6.2)
- Take Notes—Create a concept web or other type of graphic organizer to track arguments and specific claims and the supportive reasons and evidence. (RI.7.8)
- Take Notes—As you read or listen to informational text, use a T-chart to identify reasons and evidence. Put reasons on one side and evidence on the other. With a partner, discuss the soundness of the reasons, circling those reasons that are sound. Then discuss the evidence and circle all that are relevant. Discuss whether or not the amount of evidence is sufficient to support the argument and claims. (RI.7.8, SL.7.1)
- Take Notes—As you read or listen to informational text, jot down examples of the writer's or speaker's bias or use of propaganda or exaggeration. Cite several pieces of textual evidence to support your analysis. (RI.7.8, RI.7.1)
- Take Notes—Create a T-chart to differentiate between evidence and opinions placing evidence on one side and opinions on the other. Discuss the difference between the details on both sides with a partner, remembering that evidence can be facts or documentation used to support a claim. Circle the evidence on the chart if it is relevant. (RI.7.8, SL.7.1)
- Take Notes—As you read or work with arguments and claims in advertisements, look for and note any persuasive techniques used such as
    - Repetition
    - Reasons why
    - Consistency
    - Comparisons
    - Potential objections
    - Storytelling

- Card stacking
- Name calling
- Plain folks
- Transfer
- Bandwagon
- Testimonials
- "Free" or "bargain"
- Glittering generalities

- Nonlinguistic Representation—Create a concept web to illustrate an argument and claims and the supporting evidence for each argument presented on similar topics. As a class, determine and eliminate opinions and nonrelevant evidence. Determine whether or not the remaining evidence is sufficient to support the argument. Then determine which argument is the strongest argument for the topic at hand. (RI.7.8, SL.7.1)
- Cooperative Learning—With a partner, read an excerpt, interview, or selection. Your teacher will provide them for you. Write down the argument and any evidence and reasons found and decide if the claims are supported with sound reasons and relevant evidence. Highlight the relevant evidence and circle the sound reasons. Discuss with your partner whether or not there is sufficient evidence and sound reasoning to support the argument. Jot down your thoughts and be prepared to share them with the class. (RI.7.8, SL.7.1)
- Cooperative Learning—Work with a partner to evaluate and determine the authenticity and quality of a text as well as the author's qualifications and background knowledge. Create a graphic organizer that illustrates the claims and supportive evidence of an argument. Then conduct a short research project to answer the questions: is the author qualified to present the argument and is the text presented authentic? Use several sources to answer your questions. Each claim and piece of evidence presented by the author should be cited and supported using additional resources. Cite textual evidence from your sources to substantiate the author's claims and evidence with page numbers and titles of sources. Your teacher may give you specific ways to cite your information. Present your findings to the class. (RI.7.8, RI.7.1, W.7.2, W.7.7, SL.7.1)
- Cooperative Learning—After a class presentation, do a Paraphrase Passport.[2] Students should get into groups of four. The first student makes comments or observations about the argument and the claims while the others listen. The next student must paraphrase what the first student said before adding his own comments or observations about the supporting evidence. The next student paraphrases the first two students and adds his own comments or ob-

servations about the relevancy of the evidence. The last student must paraphrase what the others said and adds his or her own comments or observations about how sufficient the evidence is and makes a final conclusion that supports the argument. (RI.7.8, SL.7.1)

- Questions—Consider these questions when discussing arguments, claims, reasoning, and evidence. (RI.7.8)
    - Is the author qualified?
    - Is the author affiliated with an organization?
    - What are the author's credentials?
        - This information can be found in the text of an article or book; on the title page, book cover, or dust jacket; directly below the article title; or at the end of the article.
        - You can also check under the author's name in Biography Reference Bank, Contemporary Authors, or Biography Collection Complete.
    - Is the author's education in the subject area in which she is writing?
    - Has the author written other books or articles on the subject?
    - Is the book, article or website written in the author's field of expertise?
    - What is the author's purpose?
    - Is the information accurate?
    - Is the information valid? Is the same information found in other sources?
    - Is the information biased or objective?
        - Does the author treat his subject in a positive or negative light?
        - How are the subjects portrayed in photographs?
        - Are both sides presented?
    - Is the information current?
    - If graphs, charts or texts used numbers, can they be verified and where?
    - Are there stated sources?
- Homework and Practice—Practice tracing and evaluating arguments and claims with sound reasoning and relevant evidence. Read a selection from a mini-mystery and complete an argumentation frame based on the "argument" and "claims" presented in the text. Create and complete a table that lists the supported claims, reasons, and relevant evidence. Is there sufficient evidence to determine the guilty party, reach the same conclusions, or solve the mystery? How could the author have improved the argument or claim?

What other evidence should the author have included? Cite the page numbers of the specific text that supports the claims made in the text. Be prepared to present your evaluation to the group or class. (RI.7.8, RI.7.1, SL.7.1)

> *Five Minute Mysteries: 37 Challenging Cases of Murder and Mayhem for You to Solve* by Ken Weber (1989)
> *Hawkeye Collins and Amy Adams in the Case of the Chocolate Snatcher* by M. Masters (1983)
> *One Minute Mysteries: 65 Short Mysteries You Solve with Math!* by Eric Yoder (2010)
> *The Case of the Mysterious Dognapper* by M. Masters (2013)
> *The Case of the Video Game Smugglers* by M. Masters (2013)

- Homework and Practice—Analyze arguments and distinguish claims supported by sound reasoning and sufficient, relevant evidence as presented by classmates. Listen to the arguments and claims, reasons and evidence as presented. On your printed copy, highlight important information such as the argument or claim (main idea) in one color and evidence (supporting details) in another color. Use different colors for counterclaims and supportive evidence if it is found in the speech. Create a T-chart that lists the sound reasons on one side and the relevant evidence on the other. Indicate specific text that supports the claims. Use the information on the T-chart in group or class discussion to determine whether or not the argument and claims are supported. (RI.7.8, RI.7.1, SL.7.1)
- Homework and Practice—Look at a variety of advertisements. A good source is Ad* Access at http://library.duke.edu/digitialcollections/adaccess or you can check your local newspapers or magazines. Write an informative essay to trace and evaluate the claims in the ads and identify examples of sound reasoning and relevant evidence in an advertisement. Use a variety of sentence structures, appropriate capitalization, punctuation and spelling, precise and concise language, and figurative language where appropriate. Edit for grammar and mechanics. Cite several pieces of evidence to support your analysis. (RI.7.8, RI.7.1, W.7.2, L.7.1b–c, L.7.2, L.7.3)
- Compare and Contrast—Compare and contrast one author's presentation of events with that of another using biographies, autobiographies, and memoirs. Create a T-chart or other graphic organizer to illustrate examples of style, theme, organization, events, characters, and ideas presented. Use the information from the charts, webs, or diagrams to write a comparison and contrast essay. Use a variety of sentence structures, appropriate capitalization, punctuation and spelling, precise and concise language, and figurative language where appropriate. Edit for grammar and mechanics. Cite

several pieces of evidence to support your analysis. (RI.7.9, RI.7.1, W.7.2, L.7.1b–c, L.7.2, L.7.3)

- Use concept webs or Venn diagrams to compare and contrast information presented.
- Compare and contrast fictional characters with real people who have similar traits or actions from the same period.

- Compare and Contrast—Compare and contrast a memoir or autobiography to a biography of the same person by creating a life graph timeline for each text. On the top of the timeline illustrate and identify events that were positive and put negative events on the bottom of the timeline, all in chronological order. In class discussion, compare and contrast the two graphs, noting events that are similar to both graphs and those that are different. In your discussion, discuss possible reasons why the authors chose to emphasize different evidence or interpret facts differently. (RI.7.9, SL.7.1)
- Compare and Contrast—In an essay, compare and contrast a historical fiction text and an informational text or two informational texts based on the same period (Middle Ages, Holocaust, etc.). How are the accounts similar and different? Why would the accounts vary? Who really existed and who is fictional in the accounts? What are similar and different circumstances, traits, and actions? Create a Venn diagram to use in prewriting. Use a variety of sentence structures, appropriate capitalization, punctuation and spelling, precise and concise language, and figurative language where appropriate. Edit for grammar and mechanics. Cite several pieces of evidence to support your analysis. (RI.7.9, RI.7.1, W.7.2, L.7.1b–c, L.7.2, L.7.3)
  - Topics to consider:
    - Abigail Adams
    - Joan of Arc
    - Neil Armstrong
    - Clara Barton
    - Christopher Columbus
    - Marie Curie
    - Charles Dickens
    - Alexander Graham Bell
    - Elizabeth Blackwell
    - Emily Dickinson
    - Walt Disney
    - Frederick Douglass
    - Amelia Earhart
    - Albert Einstein
    - Anne Frank

- Benjamin Franklin
- Bill Gates
- Ulysses S. Grant
- Thomas Jefferson
- Martin Luther King Jr.
- Robert E. Lee
- Abraham Lincoln
- Dolly Madison
- Rosa Parks
- Edgar Allen Poe
- Condoleezza Rice
- Eleanor Roosevelt
- Theodore Roosevelt
- William Shakespeare
- Elizabeth Cady Stanton
- Gary Soto
- Sojourner Truth
- Harriet Tubman
- Mark Twain
- Booker T. Washington
- George Washington

- Take Notes—As you read, jot down notes about characters and events in informational and historical texts with regard to evidence presented and the interpretation of facts. Does the genre affect how the evidence is presented and the interpretation of the facts? Cite your textual evidence so you can find it for discussions. (RI.7.9, RI.7.1)
- Take Notes—With a partner, small group or as a class, create a table with 4 columns. Label the columns across "Source," "Evidence," and "Facts." Down the side of the table, label the rows "Author 1" and "Author 2." Add additional rows for other authors. Use the table to analyze how two or more authors writing about the same topic shape their presentations emphasizing different evidence or advancing different interpretations of facts. In the first column, list the text(s) used—the sources for each author. Complete the chart by entering evidence emphasized and facts advanced by each author from each source. Circle the similarities; note the differences. Discuss why the authors chose or didn't choose to write emphasizing the same evidence and advancing the same facts. (RI.7.9, SL.7.1)
- Nonlinguistic Representations—Create a two- or three-circle Venn diagram to illustrate the evidence or facts presented by different authors on the same topic. Use the diagrams for group or class discussion. (RI.7.9, SL.7.1)

- Nonlinguistic Representation—Create individual posters to illustrate the theme, characters, and facts and evidence as presented by the author from historical fiction or informational texts on the same theme. As a class, discuss the similarities and differences in the evidence and facts presented. Discuss possible reasons why each author chose to shape their information in that way. (RI.7.9, SL.7.1)
- Cooperative Learning—As a class you will do a Kagan Cooperative Learning structure called Jigsaw.[3] Your teacher will give you one of three selections by different authors on the same topic. Read and outline the selection, noting whether you have author one, two or three. Your outline should include the evidence presented and the author's interpretation of facts. Your teacher will signal you to get into author groups so that all author ones are together, author twos are together and author threes are together. Each group will discuss their outlines, checking for accuracy and completeness of information. At the next teacher signal, groups will divide into new groups. Each new group will have each author represented. Beginning with the outline for author one, share the outlines and discuss how the authors presented their information and noting similar or different interpretations of facts. Discuss possible reasons for the similarities and differences. As a group, write a conclusion about the possible reasons discussed and share it with the class. (RI.7.9, SL.7.1)
- Hypothesize and Test—Authors of informational texts do/do not emphasize different evidence or advance different interpretations of facts when writing about the same topic. Choose your hypothesis and as you read, document and cite evidence to prove or disprove your hypothesis. At the end of the year, complete a Hypothesis Worksheet (see appendix D) and present your findings to the class. (RI.7.9, RI.7.1)
- Questions—Consider the following questions when discussing evidence and facts presented by authors. (RI.7.9)
    - Do the author's qualifications affect his style?
    - Do the author's qualifications affect her interpretation of facts?
    - Do the author's qualifications determine which evidence is emphasized?
- Homework and Practice—As you read, take note of examples of the author's point of view or bias. What specific language is used that reveals the point of view or bias? Does the point of view or bias affect how the evidence is emphasized and how the facts are interpreted? Write an essay to describe the author's point of view and how it affects the evidence and the facts. Use a variety of sentence structures, appropriate capitalization, punctuation and spelling, precise and concise language, and figurative language where ap-

propriate. Edit for grammar and mechanics. Cite several pieces of evidence to support your analysis. (RI.7.9, RI.7.1, W.7.2, L.7.1b–c, L.7.2, L.7.3)
- Take Notes—As you read, take notes about how your characters are affected by the time period in which they live. (RI.7.10)
- Questions—As you read, consider and discuss responses to the following questions in small or large group situations. (RI.7.10, SL.7.1)
    - What is the genre?
    - How does the genre affect the characters? Events? Settings?
    - What is the overall theme?
    - When and where does the event take place? Is the story related to a historical event?
- Questions—Throughout the year you will read a variety of literature. To help determine books of interest, interview a book by "asking questions" about the book. (RI.7.10)
    - Look at the title and cover art if any. Does the title sound interesting?
    - Look at the author's name. Have you read any other books by the author?
    - What do you know about the author?
    - Read the blurb inside the book or on the back of the book. Does it sound interesting or similar to others you have read on the same topic?
    - What is the genre of the book? Is it a genre you generally like to read? If you don't know the genre, are there any key word to help you determine the genre such as "mystery" or "biography"?
    - Look at the cover. Are there any seals designating the book as an award-winning book?
        - Coretta Scott King Award
        - Michael L. Printz Award
        - National Book Award
        - Newbery Award
        - Young Adult Library Services Award
    - Is the text too difficult or too easy to read?
- Homework and Practice—Read and comprehend literature in the Grades 6–8 text complexity band proficiently. (RI.7.10, SL.7.1, SL.7.6)
    - Practice reading every night, self-correcting when you make mistakes.

- Stop frequently when reading and restate in your own words what you have read.
- As you read, make mental predictions about what will happen next and check to see if you were correct.
- Record stories or poems for others to hear.
- Create skits or plays based on literary text.
- Play music in the background related to theme and topics.
- Dress in costume as you read—keep it simple—wear hats, scarves, vests; something symbolic of the topic or theme.
- Role-play the main character in stories, drama, or poems.
- Memorize and present favorite passages or poems.

> *Read All About It! Great Read-Aloud Stories, Poems and Newspaper Pieces for Pre-Teens and Teens* by Jim Trelease (1993)
>
> *Reading Comprehension, Grades 7–8* by Instructional Fair (2003)
>
> *Swimming Upstream: Middle School Poems* by Kristine O'Connell George (2002)

- Homework and Practice—Vary the genres of texts you read throughout the year. Create a class chart of recommended reading. Add text titles and authors to the chart, including those read as a class and others read through independent reading. Set a goal to read two to three books from each genres in addition to those read as a class. (RI.7.10)
- Homework and Practice—To help students better visualize characters, individuals, events, and settings, incorporate a variety of visuals and experiences. (RI.7.10)
    - Attend plays or reenactments in your area.
    - Post calendar pictures, book jackets, magazine, or other printed pictures around the room that represent your current topics and refer to them when taking notes.
    - Look for original prints you could borrow from libraries or parents.
    - Create areas in the room representative of settings or events.
    - Create artifact tables—find pictures or symbolic replicas of items that represent people, characters, or events.
    - Eat a meal that would be symbolic of your theme or topic.
    - Listen to music that represents your topic during free time or played softly in the background while taking notes.
- Homework and Practice—Read aloud or listen to various grade level texts. (RI.7.10)

NOTES

1. Kagan, S., & Kagan, M. (1997). *Kagan Cooperative Learning Smart Card* (pp. 2–3). San Clemente, CA: Kagan Publishing.
2. See Kagan, S., & Kagan, M. (1997) for further information.
3. See Kagan, S., & Kagan, M. (1997) for further information.

SIX
Grade 7 Strategies and Activities for Writing

Choose literary and informational text from Grades 6–8 text exemplars selections or other appropriate grade-level selections. Grades 6–8 text exemplars are noted with an (EX).

- Compare and Contrast—Compare and contrast your argument with those of classmates on similar topics. Get into groups of similar topics and discuss your arguments in terms of logical reasoning, relevant evidence, and the use of accurate, credible sources. Create a concept web for your group to illustrate the similarities and differences in your supported evidence and reasons. If you as a group could write one argument that incorporated the best information from the concept web, how would it be different from the one you wrote? Share the concept web and suggested improvements with the class. (W.7.1, SL.7.1, SL.7.6)
- Take Notes—Use outlines or other graphic organizers to take notes on topics for arguments, informative/explanatory texts, narratives or other short research projects (W.7.1, W.7.2, W.7.3, W.7.7, W.7.10)
- Take Notes—Create T-charts to organize facts and evidence for arguments. On one side of the chart, state opinions. On the other side state supportive facts for the opinions. (W.7.1)
    - Use T-charts for ideas. On one side, list the supportive ideas. On the other side, state supportive facts, details, and examples for each idea on the other side of the chart.
- Homework and Practice—Write arguments to support claims with logical reasoning, relevant evidence, and accurate, credible sources. Use words, phrases, and clauses to create cohesion and clarify the

relationships among claim(s), reasons, and evidence. Use a variety of sentence structures, appropriate punctuation and spelling, and precise language. Use multiple print and digital sources, paraphrase and quote appropriately, and assess credibility and accuracy of sources. Use a concluding statement or section that follows from the argument presented. Draw and cite several pieces of textual evidence from informational texts to support your analysis, reflection, and research. Create a T-chart or other appropriate graphic organizer to state the claim or argument and brainstorm a list of the pros and cons of your claim. Select the best three pros or cons and discuss your choices with a classmate; consider their suggestions. Use technology to produce and publish your argument and link to and cite your sources. Edit your writing for grammar and mechanics. You may be asked to present your argument to the class emphasizing salient points with pertinent descriptions, facts, details, and examples. Include multimedia components when necessary and adapt speech to the task at hand. (W.7.1, W.7.4, W.7.5, W.7.6, W.7.8, W.7.9, RI.7.1, SL.7.1, SL.7.4, SL.7.5, SL.7.6, L.7.1b–c, L.7.2, L.7.3)

- Choose topics or ideas such as
    - The dress code should/should not be revised.
    - Students should/should not pass a reading test to get a driver's license.
    - Cell phones should/should not be allowed in class.
    - Motorcycles are/are not safe modes of transportation for students ages eighteen to twenty-one.
    - Energy drinks should/should not be sold at school.
    - Parents should/should not help students with homework.
    - Field trips should/should not be part of the educational experience.
    - Students are/are not too dependent on computers/cell phones.
    - Companies should/should not be allowed to market to middle school students.
    - Violent video games do/do not cause bad behavior.
    - Competition for grades is/is not good in middle school.
    - There is/is not a danger to communication with the advent of social media.
    - Technology has/has not affected your learning abilities.
    - Pass time should/should not be extended in your school.
    - All citizens should/should not have to pass a test on issues before voting.

- High school should/should not require community service to graduate.
- Students should/should not say the Pledge of Allegiance at school each day.
- Students who maintain a 3.8 GPA should/should not be allowed to miss extra days at school.
- There should/should not be a dress code for teachers.
- Internet chat rooms are/are not safe for middle school students.
- Classrooms should/should not be coed.
- To help brainstorm for ideas, post the topics on chart paper around the room and allow students to share their ideas or thoughts or details on the chart paper. Students can use the information to help with their arguments and evidence.

- Classmates should delineate the speaker's argument and specific claims and evaluate the soundness of the reasoning and the relevance and sufficiency of the evidence by creating a T-chart to illustrate supported reasons and relevant evidence on one side and unsupported and nonrelevant evidence on the other side of the chart. (SL.7.3)

- Homework and Practice—Create a character map for subjects of autobiographies or memoirs. Your map should identify the person, her actions, decisions, and how well the person responded to the events, actions, or decisions. Was the person justified in the actions or decisions made? Write an argument to support or criticize one or two major actions or decisions made by the person and whether or not the person was justified in the action or decision made. Support your claim with logical reasoning, relevant evidence, and accurate, credible sources. Use words, phrases, and clauses to create cohesion and clarify the relationships among claim(s), reasons, and evidence. Use a variety of sentence structures, appropriate punctuation and spelling, and precise language. Use multiple print and digital sources, paraphrase and quote appropriately, and assess credibility and accuracy of sources. Use a concluding statement or section that follows from the argument presented. Create a T-chart or other appropriate graphic organizer to state the claim or argument and brainstorm a list of the pros and cons of your claim. Select the best three pros or cons and discuss your choices with a classmate; consider their suggestions. Use technology to produce and publish your argument and link to and cite your sources. Draw and cite several pieces of textual evidence from informational texts to support your analysis, reflection, and research. Edit your writing for grammar and mechanics. You may be asked to present your argument to the class emphasizing salient points with pertinent descriptions, facts, details, and examples. Include multimedia components when necessary and adapt speech to the task at hand. (W.7.1, W.7.4, W.7.5, W.7.8, W.7.9, RI.7.1, SL.7.1, SL.7.4, SL.7.5, SL.7.6, L.7.1b–c, L.7.2, L.7.3)

- Classmates should delineate the speaker's argument and specific claims and evaluate the soundness of the reasoning and the relevance and sufficiency of the evidence by creating a T-chart to illustrate supported reasons and relevant evidence on one side and unsupported and nonrelevant evidence on the other side of the chart. (SL.7.3)

- Homework and Practice—Think about a book you have recently read. Write an argument that your book (use the title of the book) does/does not mirror the events of life. Create a graphic organizer of events, characters, and decisions made as well as logical reasons and relevant evidence. Review the text if necessary. Ask a partner to check your claim and evidence. Write an argument to support or criticize your claim(s). Support your claim(s) with logical reasoning and relevant evidence. Use words, phrases, and clauses to create cohesion and clarify the relationships among claim(s), reasons, and evidence. Use a variety of sentence structures, appropriate punctuation and spelling, and precise language. Use multiple print and digital sources, paraphrase and quote appropriately, and assess credibility and accuracy of sources. Use a concluding statement or section that follows from the argument presented. Draw and cite several pieces of textual evidence from informational texts to support your analysis, reflection, and research. Edit your writing for grammar and mechanics. You may be asked to present your argument to the class emphasizing salient points with pertinent descriptions, facts, details, and examples. Include multimedia components when necessary and adapt speech to the task at hand. (W.7.1, W.7.4, W.7.5, W.7.8. W.7.9, RI.7.1, SL.7.1, SL.7.4, SL.7.5, SL.7.6, L.7.1b–c, L.7.2, L.7.3)

  - Classmates should delineate the speaker's argument and specific claims and evaluate the soundness of the reasoning and the relevance and sufficiency of the evidence by creating a T-chart to illustrate supported reasons and relevant evidence on one side and unsupported and nonrelevant evidence on the other side of the chart. (SL.7.3)

- Homework and Practice—Select a poem or drama and write an argument to support or oppose the idea that the structure or form contributes to the meaning. Support your claim(s) with logical reasoning and relevant evidence. Use words, phrases, and clauses to create cohesion and clarify the relationships among claim(s), reasons, and evidence. Use a variety of sentence structures, appropriate punctuation and spelling, and precise language. Use multiple print and digital sources, paraphrase and quote appropriately, and assess credibility and accuracy of sources. Use a concluding statement or section that follows from the argument presented. Draw and cite several pieces of textual evidence from informational texts to support your analysis, reflection, and research. Edit your writing for grammar and mechanics. You may be asked to present your argument to the class emphasizing salient points with pertinent descriptions, facts, details, and examples. Include multimedia components when necessary and adapt speech to the task at hand. (W.7.1, W.7.4, W.7.5, W.7.8, W.7.9, SL.7.1, SL.7.4, SL.7.5, SL.7.6, L.7.1b–c, L.7.2, L.7.3)

- Classmates should delineate the speaker's argument and specific claims and evaluate the soundness of the reasoning and the relevance and sufficiency of the evidence by creating a T-chart to illustrate supported reasons and relevant evidence on one side and unsupported and nonrelevant evidence on the other side of the chart. (SL.7.3)

- Homework and Practice—Write and present persuasive presentations that use clear logical arguments and relevant evidence. Recognize and address opposing points of view in your paper. Use words, phrases, and clauses to create cohesion and clarify the relationships among claim(s), reasons, and evidence. Use a variety of sentence structures, appropriate punctuation and spelling, and precise language. Use multiple print and digital sources, paraphrase and quote appropriately, and assess credibility and accuracy of sources. Use a concluding statement or section that follows from the argument presented. Emphasize salient points with pertinent descriptions, facts, details, and examples. Include multimedia components when necessary and adapt speech to the task at hand. Draw and cite several pieces of textual evidence from informational texts to support your analysis, reflection, and research. Edit your writing for grammar and mechanics. (W.7.1, W.7.4, W.7.5, W.7.8, W.7.9, RI.7.1, SL.7.1, SL.7.4, SL.7.5, SL.7.6, L.7.1b–c, L.7.2, L.7.3)

  - Classmates should delineate the speaker's argument and specific claims and evaluate the soundness of the reasoning and the relevance and sufficiency of the evidence by creating a T-chart to illustrate supported reasons and relevant evidence on one side and unsupported and nonrelevant evidence on the other side of the chart. (SL.7.3)

- Topics could include
    - Additional seventh grade elective classes
    - Extended pass time between classes
    - No more than two hours of assigned homework at night
    - Convince principal to allow student council to host ice cream social for fundraiser
    - Allow background music while studying
    - New choices for school lunch
    - Connecting grades to attendance
    - Increase/decrease the number of school days per year
    - Food or drink in the classrooms
    - A rule you would like to change
    - Chocolate or vanilla milk at lunch
    - Shorter school days
    - Longer lunch time
    - Mandatory community service for middle school students
- Take Notes—Create a table on a class spreadsheet or post on the wall to identify texts and authors' purposes. Create columns labeled "Inform," "Entertain," "Persuade," "Instruct," and "Retell." As you read, note in the appropriate column the title and author's name of the text. Refer to the chart for future writing assignments. (W.7.2, W.7.3)
- Nonlinguistic Representations—As you read this year, keep track on a large wall map made in class of the countries, states, or cities you read about. Select a country, state, or city you want to know more about. Talk with a partner and ask, If you could go to this place, what three things would you want to know? Conduct research to determine information about the country and culture and to answer the questions. Draw and cite several pieces of textual evidence from informational text to support your analysis and research. Use multiple print and digital sources, paraphrase and quote appropriately, and assess credibility and accuracy of sources. Create a travel brochure or poster to illustrate the answers to your questions. Add copy to go along with your brochure where needed. Share your travel brochure with the class. Discuss as a class how the main ideas and supporting details presented in the brochure or poster clarify the topic. (W.7.2, W.7.8, RI.7.1, SL.7.1, SL.7.2)
- Homework and Practice—Research the relationship between author's lives and what they write about. Write an essay to answer this question: Why do you think the author writes about _____? Cite several pieces of textual evidence to support your analysis of what the text says and infers. Check biographies, autobiographies,

memoirs, letters, or interviews. Use a variety of sentence structures, appropriate punctuation and spelling, precise language and appropriate transitions. Use multiple print and digital sources, paraphrase and quote appropriately, and assess credibility and accuracy of sources. Provide a concluding statement or section that follows from and supports the information or explanation presented. Edit your writing for grammar and mechanics. (W.7.2, W.7.4, W.7.5, W.7.7, W.7.8, RI.7.1, L.7.1b–c, L.7.2, L.7.3)

- Homework and Practice—Write an informative text in the form of a PowerPoint biography of a person of interest. Include introductory, timeline, conclusion, and reference slides. Additional slides will address the subject's accomplishments. Develop the topic with relevant facts, definitions, concrete details, quotations, or other relevant information. Add pictures, photos, clip art, audio, video, and other multimedia and visual components. Use a variety of sentence structures, appropriate punctuation and spelling, precise language, and appropriate transitions in the copy of the slides. Use multiple print and digital sources, paraphrase and quote appropriately, and assess credibility and accuracy of sources. Provide a concluding statement or section that follows from and supports the information or explanation presented. Prepare slide to cite several pieces of textual evidence. Edit the text in your slides for grammar and mechanics. Present your PowerPoint biography to the class. (W.7.2, W.7.4, W.7.5, W.7.8, RI.7.1, L.7.1b–c, L.7.2, L.7.3)
- Homework and Practice—Write informative/explanatory texts or reports on various topics. Develop the topic with relevant facts, definitions, concrete details, quotations, or other relevant information. Use a variety of sentence structures, appropriate punctuation and spelling, and precise language. Use multiple print and digital sources, paraphrase and quote appropriately, and assess credibility and accuracy of sources. Provide a concluding statement or section that follows from and supports the information or explanation presented. Edit your writing for grammar and mechanics. Cite several pieces of textual evidence in your writing. (W.7.2, W.7.4, W.7.5, W.7.8, RI.7 1, L.7.1b–c, L.7.2, L.7.3)
  - Topics could include
    - The proper way to pack a bag for vacation
    - How to prevent home fires
    - How to prepare specific foods
    - How advertising messages are tailored to increase sales
    - The importance of honesty in a friendship
    - What is it like to be the middle child?
    - What is it like to be in the middle grade in middle school?

- The proudest moment of your life
- The strangest thing to ever happen to you
- The story of how your school was founded
- Description of life in another country
- The Seven Wonders of the World
- Roadside attractions in your town
- How to organize a closet
- How to make fishing lures
- The impact of media on society
- How to collect sports cards

- Homework and Practice—Write directions for someone else explaining how to write compound, complex, and compound-complex sentences; use commas to separate coordinate adjectives; and how to use Greek or Latin affixes and roots as clues to the meaning of new words. (W.7.2, W.7.10, L.7.1b, L.7.2a, L.7.4b)
- Homework and Practice—Conduct research to answer the question: If I was in seventh grade during the Revolutionary War, how would my life be different? Write and informative/explanatory essay to develop the topic with relevant facts, definitions, concrete details, quotations, or other relevant information. Use a variety of sentence structures, appropriate punctuation and spelling, and precise language. Use multiple print and digital sources, paraphrase and quote appropriately, and assess credibility and accuracy of sources. Provide a concluding statement or section that follows from and supports the information or explanation presented. Edit your writing for grammar and mechanics. Cite several pieces of textual evidence in your writing. (W.7.2, W.7.4, W.7.5, W.7.8, RI.7 1, L.7.1b–c, L.7.2, L.7.3)
- Compare and Contrast—Write a bio-poem for a favorite author or person you have read about. You may need to do a little research about your author or person. Get with a partner who wrote about the same author or person of interest and compare and contrast the information in your bio-poems. Complete a Venn diagram to illustrate the similarities and differences. (W.7.3, SL.7.1)
- Compare and Contrast—Your teacher will collect several calendars that have scenic pictures on them. You will have a choice of three photos to write a short story about as though you lived and worked there or visited there. What do you do? Where is the name of the "town"? What are the points of interest? If you explore the town, what do you find? Use effective technique such as dialogue, pacing, and description; relevant descriptive detail, and well-structured detail. Use a variety of transition words, phrases, and clauses to convey sequence in addition to precise words and phrases, relevant descriptive details, and sensory language. Edit your short story for

grammar and mechanics. You may be asked to share your story with the class and/or publish your writing. When all stories have been completed, let groups get to together who used the same calendar picture to compare and contrast the details. Create a concept web for each group to illustrate the similarities and differences. (W.7.3, W.7.4, W.7.5, W.7.6, W.7.10, SL.7.1, SL.7.6, L.7.1b–c, L.7.2, L.7.3)

- You can also write poems based on the calendar pictures. Use rhyme, imagery, personification, alliteration, onomatopoeia, and figurative language. Choose from

    Acrostics
    Cinquain
    Concrete
    Free verse
    Haiku
    Limerick
    Sonnets

- Take Notes—As you read or participate in class discussions, take note of interesting facts, people or places for future use in narrative writings. Jot down settings and interesting events that pique your interest, too. (W.7.3)
- Nonlinguistic Representations—Role-play a major day in the life of a person you have read about. Prepare a skit entitled "A Day in the Life of ____." Cite and use multiple print and digital sources, paraphrase and quote appropriately, and assess credibility and accuracy of sources. Create a content web or outline or other appropriate organizer to organize your thoughts and list any supportive materials you will need. What would that person say and do? Why is that day so important? Practice your presentation before you present it to the class. (W.7.3, W.7.8, RI.7.1, SL.7.1, SL.7.6)
- Questions—Ask questions to spark interest in narrative writing. You might post several questions on chart paper and post around the classroom. Students read and respond to the questions as they walk around the room. Students can use the information on the charts in their writing. (W.7.3)

    - What if you could run the school for the day?
    - What if you won the lottery?
    - What if you your pets could talk?
    - What if you were the principal/teacher for the day?
    - What if you could travel to anywhere in the world?
    - What would you do if you could be the president?
    - If you could fly, where would you go? What would you see and do?

- If you could trade places with anyone for a day, who would it be, where would it be, what would you do?
- What would you do if you had no TV, video games, computers, or cell phones for a week?

- Homework and Practice—Read an autobiography, biography, or memoir. Write a news story about your subject as though you interviewed your subject using information from your text. Add dialogue, description, and characters as needed. Use a variety of transition words, phrases, and clauses to convey sequence in addition to precise words and phrases, relevant descriptive details, and sensory language. Edit your writing for grammar and mechanics. Work together and use technology to publish a class newspaper with all of the news stories. (W.7.3, W.7.4, W.7.5, W.7.6, SL.7.1, L.7.1b–c, L.7.2, L.7.3)
- Homework and Practice—Create a set of postcards you would send to a friend you met on your last vacation. You cannot speak on the phone so you will have to write to each other. You want to tell each other about interesting places to visit in your home towns. Create at least three cards written to the friend and three responses from them. Use a half sheet of white copy paper for each card. On one side, create an illustration about an interesting place to visit in your town. On the back, write to your friend to describe the illustration and update her on events since your last meeting or postcard. Be sure to save room for the address as well. Share your postcards with the class. (W.7.3, W.7.10, SL.7.1)
- Homework and Practice—Write a children's story with settings, dialogue, plot/conflict, characters, and events. Use sensory details and descriptive and figurative language. The story should teach a lesson, a value, or moral, and should be illustrated. Use a variety of transition words, phrases, and clauses to convey sequence. Provide a conclusion that follows from and reflects the narrated experiences or events. Your teacher may give you other specific guidelines. Publish your stories and create a class anthology. Stories will be shared in the class or with other grade levels. (W.7.3, W.7.4, W.7.5, W.7.6, SL.7.1, L.7.1b–c, L.7.2, L.7.3)
- Homework and Practice—Write narratives to develop real or imagined experiences or events using effective technique such as dialogue, pacing and description; relevant descriptive detail, and well-structured detail. Use a variety of transition words, phrases, and clauses to convey sequence in addition to precise words and phrases, relevant descriptive details, and sensory language. Edit your narratives for grammar and mechanics. You may be asked to share your narrative with the class and/or publish your writing.

(W.7.3, W.7.4, W.7.5, W.7.6, W.7.10, SL.7.1, SL.7.6, L.7.1b–c, L.7.2, L.7.3)

- Topics could include
    - You made a discovery that will make you rich and famous. What did you discover? Where was the discovery made and how? What will change because of the discovery for you and others?
    - If you could meet anyone, who would it be and why? Write a narrative to describe the person and your meeting. Where do you meet and what do you talk about?
    - You are lost in the desert. What three things would you want with you and why? How do you use them to help you get back to civilization?
    - Write a letter to your hero. Who is it? Why is the person important to you? Why do you look up to that person? What would you do if you ever met your hero?
    - You have the opportunity to change school lunches. What would you change and why?
    - Write a letter to your favorite author. What would you say? What would you want to know? What would you want the author to know about you?
    - You have just previewed a movie everyone is talking about. Write the questions and answers for the interview in Q&A form to convince others to go see the movie. Don't forget to describe who, what, where, when and how, but don't give away the ending. You may be asked to share your "interview" with the class.
- Homework and Practice—Write an acrostic poem to develop a real or imagined experience or event. (W.7.3)
    - Try the acrostic poem creator: www.netrover.com/~kingskid/poetry/acrostictrace.html
- Homework and Practice—Select a character or real person you have read about. Write the name of the character or person down the side of a page. Write a poem, either free verse or rhyming, about the character or person. The first word of each line begins with the letter at the beginning of the line. The poem can be done as a class exercise, with students taking turns adding a line, one at a time, or it can be written in small groups or by individuals. Poems can be shared in the class. (W.7.3, SL.7.1, SL.7.6)
    - If all students write about the same character or person, poems could be compared and contrasted in class discussions.

- Write a poem about a person who has been important in your life.
- Homework and Practice—As poems are written about various topics throughout the year, make copies of them, and create a class anthology of poetry. Illustrations may also be added to poems. (W.7.3, W.7.4, W.7.6)
- Homework and Practice—Write a dramatic interpretation for a historical fiction character or someone else from an informational text. Focus on one conflict of the character or person. It should accurately represent facts and events you read about. Use effective technique such as dialogue, pacing, and description; relevant descriptive detail, and well-structured detail. Use a variety of transition words, phrases, and clauses to convey sequence in addition to precise words and phrases, relevant descriptive details, and sensory language. Edit your writing for grammar and mechanics. Prepare a video presentation to share with the class. (W.7.3, W.7.4, W.7.5, W.7.6, W.7.10, SL.7.1, SL.7.6, L.7.1b–c, L.7.2, L.7.3)
- Homework and Practice—Write your own mystery. Create a main character. Choose and describe an interesting setting; create a mysterious event or puzzle to be solved. What events will happen to your character as he or she tries to solve the mystery? What will your cliffhanger be? How will your character solve the puzzle? Brainstorm ideas with a partner and jot ideas on a content web to help you organize your thoughts. Add visuals to your writing. Use effective technique such as dialogue, pacing and description; relevant descriptive detail, and well-structured detail. Use a variety of transition words, phrases, and clauses to convey sequence in addition to precise words and phrases, relevant descriptive details, and sensory language. Edit your mystery for grammar and mechanics. You may be asked to share your narrative with the class and/or publish your writing. (W.7.3, W.7.4, W.7.5, W.7.6, W.7.10, SL.7.1, SL.7.6, L.7.1b–c, L.7.2, L.7.3)
  - Role-play your mystery with classmates adding multimedia components and visuals where appropriate.
- Homework and Practice—Write a prequel to your favorite story. What elements of the story and characters would you need to include? What new characters would you create? Remember your prequel must end where your favorite story begins. Use effective technique such as dialogue, pacing, and description; relevant descriptive detail, and well-structured detail. Use a variety of transition words, phrases and clauses to convey sequence in addition to precise words and phrases, relevant descriptive details, and sensory language. Edit your narratives for grammar and mechanics. You

may be asked to share your narrative with the class and/or publish your writing. (W.7.3, W.7.4, W.7.5, W.7.6, W.7.10, SL.7.1, SL.7.6, L.7.1b–c, L.7.2, L.7.3)
- Homework and Practice—Think about a minor character from a story, play, drama, or poem. Write the "rest of the story" for that minor character. What happened to him or her? You need to create a setting and a problem that the major character couldn't solve in the original story. Does this change the way he or she was seen originally? What elements of the story need to stay the same: What needs to be changed? How old is the character now? Your story should end with "and now you know the rest of the story." Use effective technique such as dialogue, pacing, and description; relevant descriptive detail, and well-structured detail. Use a variety of transition words, phrases, and clauses to convey sequence in addition to precise words and phrases, relevant descriptive details, and sensory language. Edit your story for grammar and mechanics. You may be asked to share your narrative with the class and/or publish your writing. (W.7.3, W.7.4, W.7.5, W.7.6, W.7.10, SL.7.1, SL.7.6, L.7.1b–c, L.7.2, L.7.3)
  - Record or role-play your story.
- Homework and Practice—Write magazine or feature articles for a class publication. Conduct research on topics of interest. Conduct interviews of experts to add interest to your articles. Use effective technique such as dialogue, pacing and description; relevant descriptive detail, and well-structured detail. Use a variety of transition words, phrases and clauses to convey sequence in addition to precise words and phrases, relevant descriptive details, and sensory language. Edit your articles for grammar and mechanics. You may be asked to share your narrative with the class and/or publish your writing. (W.7.3, W.7.4, W.7.5, W.7.6, W.7.10, SL.7.1, SL.7.6, L.7.1b–c, L.7.2, L.7.3)
- Homework and Practice—Write your memoir. Think about something you want to remember forever—something you learned that changed the way you think. You will be telling "your" story—not "a" story. Use sensory and personal details and share your thoughts and feelings. Create a time line to identify several small events or many details about one major event. Use the timeline to help you organize your thoughts. Your teacher may give you a specific format to follow. Use effective technique such as dialogue, pacing, and description; relevant descriptive detail, and well-structured detail. Use a variety of transition words, phrases, and clauses to convey sequence in addition to precise words and phrases, relevant descriptive details, and sensory language. Edit your narratives for grammar and mechanics. You may be asked to share your me-

moir with the class and/or publish your writing. (W.7.3, W.7.4, W.7.5, W.7.6, W.7.10, SL.7.1, SL.7.6, L.7.1b–c, L.7.2, L.7.3)

- Topics to consider include
    - When you realized you were no longer a child
    - The best birthday present you ever received
    - The saddest time of your life
    - The time you chose to do something different from everyone else
    - The time you figured out something you never knew before
    - Your biggest success
    - The time when someone changed the way you think about an issue
    - Something you used to do when you were little
- Homework and Practice—Choose a "can" and use the elements inside to write a mystery or a story. Your teacher will have several cans from which to choose. Look at the four to five elements in the can—use your imagination—and be creative! (Teachers, you can put almost anything in the cans—photos, toys, odd game pieces, playing cards, calendar pictures for settings and details—you can be creative, too!) Use effective technique such as dialogue, pacing, and description; relevant descriptive detail, and well-structured detail. Use a variety of transition words, phrases and clauses to convey sequence in addition to precise words and phrases, relevant descriptive details, and sensory language. Edit your stories or mysteries for grammar and mechanics. You may be asked to share your narrative with the class and/or publish your writing. (W.7.3, W.7.4, W.7.5, W.7.6, W.7.10, SL.7.1, SL.7.6, L.7.1b–c, L.7.2, L.7.3)
- Homework and Practice—Write and prepare an autobiography in PowerPoint form. Include slides for your name, birthdate, how you got your name, names of parents/guardians, siblings names and ages, favorite pets, favorite hobbies, interests, clubs, activities, or sports. Who is your role model? What historical events happened on your birthdate? With whom do you share your birthday? Prepare a multimedia presentation that includes word documents and PowerPoint slides. Add appropriate visuals and multimedia components. Present your PowerPoint to the class. (W.7.3, W.7.4, W.7.5, W.7.6, W.7.10, SL.7.1, SL.7.6, L.7.1b–c, L.7.2, L.7.3)
- Homework and Practice—Write your own science fiction story based on "what if . . ." Use effective technique such as dialogue, pacing and description; relevant descriptive detail, and well-structured detail. Use a variety of transition words, phrases, and clauses to convey sequence in addition to precise words and phrases, rele-

Strategies and Activities for Writing 95

vant descriptive details, and sensory language. Edit your stories or mysteries for grammar and mechanics. You may be asked to share your narrative with the class and/or publish your writing. (W.7.3, W.7.4, W.7.5, W.7.6, W.7.10, SL.7.1, SL.7.6, L.7.1b–c, L.7.2, L.7.3)

- Topics could include:
    - What if your mom/dad/teacher/best friend was an alien?
    - What if you were stuck in an elevator and were transported to another planet?
    - What if animals could talk?
    - What if people lived underwater?
    - What if you could be invisible?
    - What if everyone looked the same?
    - What if everyone dressed the same?
    - What if you found an alien in your class?
    - What if you found a magic wand?
    - What if you suddenly couldn't talk?
    - What if there were no rules at school?
    - What if you could fly?
    - What if you had a super power?
    - What if you could travel back in time?
    - What if you traveled through a black hole?
    - What if you were trapped inside a computer?
    - What if you couldn't remember who you are/where you lived?
    - What if your family had to move to the moon?
    - What if you could have any job in the world, what would it be?
- Take Notes—As you read various genres, take notes about the style, organization, and purposes for writing found in each genre. (W.7.4)
- Compare and Contrast—Compare and contrast a first draft to your final draft. Explain to a partner how and why you planned, revised, edited, and rewrote the first draft to strengthen your writing. (W.7.5, SL.7.1)
- Compare and Contrast—Conduct research into various ways to approach a topic that have been used by others. Create a web or other appropriate organizer to illustrate the various approaches. Cite examples of the approaches found using titles and page numbers or use a citation format provided by your teacher. Share your findings with the class. (W.7.5, RL.7.1, RI.7.1, SL.7.1)
- Take Notes—Take notes as you talk with peers and teachers about expanding ideas to improve your writing. (W.7.5, SL.7.1)

- Take Notes—To improve your writing, make and note observations about things around you—the settings, people, places, events—for use in possible current or future stories or topics. (W.7.5)
- Take Notes—Create a class chart to display editing and proofreading checklists for all to use when working in small groups or as a class. The chart will also remind you of what you need to check when editing and revising your work. (W.7.5)
- Questions—Ask questions of peers and teachers when planning, revising, editing, rewriting, or trying new approaches. (W.7.5, SL.7.1)
- Homework and Practice—Rewrite text into a different genre. You could change a memoir into a poem; a biography into a narrative story; a mystery into fantasy. Use effective technique such as dialogue, pacing, and description; relevant descriptive detail, and well-structured detail. Use a variety of transition words, phrases, and clauses to convey sequence in addition to precise words and phrases, relevant descriptive details, and sensory language. Edit your stories or mysteries for grammar and mechanics. You may be asked to share your narrative with the class and/or publish your writing. (W.7.3, W.7.4, W.7.5, W.7.6, W.7.10, SL.7.1, SL.7.6, L.7.1b–c, L.7.2, L.7.3)
    - Compare and Contrast—Create a table or T-chart to show what you kept the same and what you changed.
- Take Notes—Use class or individual spreadsheets, charts, or other print or digital sources to take notes. (W.7.6)
- Cooperative Learning—Interact and collaborate with others while using technology to communicate, produce and publish. (W.7.6)
    - Write and respond to emails as allowed in your district.
    - Use online learning programs as allowed in your district.
- Homework and Practice—Use technology, including the Internet, to produce and publish writing and link to and cite sources as well as interact and collaborate with others. (W.7.6, SL.7.1)
    - Use keyboarding skills to draft, revise, edit, and publish your work.
    - Use computers and scanners to create and edit documents and to add photos or images.
    - Use digital dictionaries, a thesaurus, and spell check when writing and editing.
- Questions—When conducting short research projects, ask a variety of relevant questions. See the stem statements in appendix C. (W.7.7)

- Use interviews, books, articles, photos, illustrations, and the Internet to locate and verify answers to questions.
- Use multiple online sites and resources for your research.

- Homework and Practice—Use concise writing and several resources when responding to a prompt, refocusing the inquiry when needed. (W.7.7)
- Compare and Contrast—Compare and contrast information in print and digital resources on the same topic using a T-Chart, Venn diagram, or other appropriate organizer. Compare and contrast three or more print or digital resources to assess the credibility and accuracy of each source. Is the information the same? What information is different? Can you determine why the information would be different? Does one resource seem to be more credible than the other? Share your diagram with a partner or small group. (W.7.8, SL.7.1)
- Summarizing—Summarize texts from print and digital sources including only appropriate and important details. Appropriately cite your sources. (W.7.8, RI.7.1)
- Take Notes—Quote or paraphrase the data and conclusions of others while avoiding plagiarism; create a bibliography of references according to the format provided by your teacher. (W.7.8, RI.7.1)
    - Remember to cite and credit downloaded materials from interactive media.
    - Note sources of information to be used in bibliography.
    - Use references and footnote when necessary.
    - Take notes to organize data and record information.
- Take Notes—Assess the credibility of each source. Take note of the author's qualifications and credentials. Has the author been peer reviewed? Are there clues to the author's bias? Is the information current and comparable to other sources? Does the author include a bibliography and citations? Are there mechanical errors? If using a website, is it a commercial, educational, governmental, or nonprofit site? (W.7.8)
- Cooperative Learning—When considering several resources on the same topic for a group project, divide up the resources among the group. Skim the information and taking turns, paraphrase the data and any conclusions for the group. Decide which resources you want to use based on the paraphrases. Cite your evidence for future use in your group project. (W.7.8, RI.7.1)
- Homework and Practice—Practice quoting and paraphrasing data and conclusions of others following formats provided by your teacher. (W.7.8)

- Homework and Practice—Write for extended time frames, a range of tasks and purposes, and various audiences. Conduct research when necessary. Edit your writing and be prepared to present your writing to the class. (W.7.10, SL.7.1, SL.7.6, L.7.1b–c, L.7.2, L.7.3)
    - Write a variety of short stories including.
    - Write a biography about a relative or friend.
    - Write feature articles for a class magazine. Your teacher may provide specific topics related to your school.
    - Write various types of poetry and compile into an individual anthology. Write poems to include cinquains, circle poems, concrete poems, free verse, haiku, and limericks.

SEVEN
Grade 7 Strategies and Activities for Speaking and Listening

Choose literary or informational text from Grades 6–8 text exemplars selections or other appropriate grade-level selections. Grades 6–8 text exemplars are noted with an (EX).

- Take Notes—Use sticky notes or tags to mark texts and to find information for class or group discussions. Refer to the notes or tags on the topic, text, or issue to probe and reflect on ideas under discussion. (SL.7.1)
- Take Notes—Use the two-column note format to indicate specific text citations in class notes. Put notes on the right half and citations on the left. Use appropriate formats for citations. (SL.7.1, RL.7.1, RI.7.1)
- Take Notes—Take notes in a format comfortable for you as you listen in group or class discussions. Formulate questions before and during presentations, looking for answers in texts during discussions. (SL.7.1)
- Take Notes—Create a journal to write reflections on a daily basis on key ideas and perspectives. (SL.7.1)
- Take Notes—To track progress toward specific goals and deadlines, help students to set SMART goals for group projects. Create an organizer for students to complete. See a sample SMART Goal form in appendix F. (SL.7.1b)
- Cooperative Learning—Practice ways to "get the floor" in group or class discussions. Follow rules for collegial discussions, set goals, and deadlines, defining individual roles as needed. Your teacher may have specific roles and guidelines for you to follow. (SL.7.1)

- You can use talking stones or chips—students begin discussion with three to four stones or chips and gives one up each time they add to the discussion. When stones or chips are gone, they must wait until all others have contributed. If you want to limit discussion, give one stone or chip to each student. You can also use a timekeeper to limit the length of contributions to discussions so you have time for all to contribute.
- You can also toss a ball—and one student speaks. If others want to contribute, the first student tosses the ball to another student. This continues until all who want to contribute have the opportunity to do so.
- You can use playing cards to "stack the deck." Students are given a card and contribute according to their card. Begin with aces and proceed down through the deck ending with deuces.
- Anticipate disagreements and use language to prevent conflict; solve issues without conflict or anger.
- Use the Kagan Cooperative Learning strategy of Paraphrase Passport[1] to review key ideas and multiple perspectives. Students should get into groups of four. The first student makes comments or observations about a topic (such as why they would or would not visit the country presented) while the others listen. The next student must paraphrase what the first student said before adding his or her own comments or observations. The process continues around the group until all have paraphrased and contributed. (SL.7.1)
    - Paraphrase Passport can also be used to review key ideas expressed and demonstrate understanding of multiple perspectives in small group discussions.
    - Allow students to suggest ways to "get the floor" such as by raising hands, talk in a circle sequentially, or birthdates.
    - Allow all to contribute before changing the subject.
- Questions—Use and respond to stem questions from Appendix C with elaboration and detail by making comments that contribute to the topic, text or issue under discussion. (SL.7.1)
- Homework and Practice—When presenting verbal arguments, use vocabulary appropriate to the argument and support the argument with sufficient, relevant evidence and sound reasoning. (SL.7.1)
- Take Notes—Note or summarize specific information gained from illustrations or graphics. Do the illustrations and graphics help to tell the story or are they distracting? Cite the page number of the

illustration or graphic for easy retrieval in group or class discussion. (SL.7.2, SL.7.1, RL.7.1, RI.7.1)
- Take Notes—Make note as to how well the print, text features, illustrations and graphics work together in the text as a whole to convey meaning or clarify the topic, text or issue. (SL.7.2)
- Take Notes—Make note of the specific information you get from photos, audio, animation, illustrations, fonts and colors. How well do they contribute to the meaning or clarify the topic, text or issue under study? (SL.7.2)
- Questions—Consider the following questions in group discussions. (SL.7.2)
    - Describe how important it is to have information presented in numerous ways (e.g., visually, quantitatively, orally)
    - How well would you comprehend main ideas and supporting details if they were only presented in one format?
- Homework and Practice—Use a SQRRR frame. Survey the chapter headings, section titles and headings, subheadings, illustrations, captions and graphics. Reword the titles and headings into questions and predict what you will read about. Be prepared to share how the illustrations, captions and graphics contribute to the topic, text or issue at hand. (SL.7.2, SL.7.1)
- Summarize—In small groups, give oral summaries of arguments and specific claims, identifying the claims that are supported by sound reasons and relevant and sufficient evidence. (SL.7.3)
- Take Notes—Create a three-column table for each argument presented in class. In the first column, identify the specific claims presented. In the second column, identify the supportive reasons for each claim, and in the third column, list the evidence for each reason. Circle all reasons that are sound and circle all evidence that is relevant. Discuss and evaluate your findings for each argument as a class. Is the evidence sufficient? (SL.7.3, SL.7.1)
- Questions—Consider the following questions when delineating arguments and claims. (SL.7.3)
    - Is a convincing argument presented?
    - Is the writer's position clearly stated?
    - Are sound reasons given and supported with appropriate and sufficient evidence?
    - Is the evidence presented relevant and sufficient?
    - Is there evidence of bias in the presentation?
- Homework and Practice—As you listen to media messages, identify and discuss instances of bias in the media messages. Try to determine the author's purpose in the bias. Discuss how the messages affect you as a middle school student. Teachers, there are

several sites from which you can choose various media messages. Please check the site prior to use in the classroom as sites do change. (SL.7.3)

> www.educationworld.com/a_lesson/lesson/lesson158.shtml. You can find several ideas here about lessons for online advertising that targets kids.
> www.ehow.com/info_12102253_advertising-activities-middle-school.html
> www.webenglishteacher.com/media-ads.html. This is a great list to help you find media and advertising resources.

- Homework and Practice—Prepare and present arguments to the class. Practice deductive reasoning by using a variety of mysteries for kids based on the claims and evidence in the books. Your teacher may provide a specific format for you to follow. Practice your argument in front of a mirror, friend, or family member prior to presenting in class. Use appropriate eye contact, volume, and pronunciation. (SL.7.4, SL.7.6)

  > *Almost Perfect Crimes: Mini-Mysteries for You to Solve* by Hy Conrad (1995)
  > *Great Quick-solve Whodunit Puzzles: Mini-Mysteries for You to Solve* by Jim Sukach (1999)
  > *Great Book of Whodunit Puzzles: Mini-Mysteries of You to Solve* by Falcon Travis (1993)
  > *CSI Expert!: Forensic Science for Kids* by Karen Schulz (2008)

- Homework and Practice—Prepare and present persuasive presentations using clear and logical arguments. Focus on salient points and use pertinent descriptions, facts, and details. Use appropriate presentation skills. Your teacher will provide a format for you to follow. (SL.7.4, SL.7.6)

    - Use topics listed for writing or other appropriate topics as listed in chapter 6 or others such as
        - Droopy pants should not be allowed in school.
        - Teens should be required to take parenting classes.
        - Kids should get paid for grades.
        - Free speech should have limitations.
        - Penmanship is important.
        - Etiquette should be taught and reinforced at school.
        - Internet access should remain free.
        - All schools should implement programs on bullying.
        - Students should be allowed to pray in school.
        - There should be a mandatory entrance and exit exam for high school.

- Homework and Practice—Include multimedia components and visual displays in presentations to clarify claims and findings and emphasize salient points. (SL.7.5)
  - Search Microsoft.com for directions on how to add sound, movies, and animation to PowerPoint presentations or Word documents.
- Nonlinguistic Presentations—Role-play a scene from favorite stories or poems. (SL.7.6)
  - Memorize and present a specific piece of nonfiction or fiction or present a dramatic reading.
- Nonlinguistic Presentations—Record stories, poems, speeches, or other appropriate readings for others to listen to. (SL.7.6)
- Homework and Practice—Practice using your voice to convey your purpose or stance; enunciate clearly; and use appropriate rate so you are understood. (SL.7.6)

NOTE

1. Kagan, S., & Kagan, M. (1997). *Kagan Cooperative Learning Smart Card* (pp. 2–3). San Clemente, CA: Kagan Publishing.

EIGHT

Grade 7 Strategies and Activities for Language

Choose literary or informational text from Grades 6–8 text exemplars selections or other appropriate grade level selections. Grades 6–8 exemplars are noted with an (EX).

- Take Notes—As you read, look for phrases and clauses and discuss their functions in the sentences. Write sentences similar to the examples for practice. Share your sentences with a partner and check for accuracy. (L.7.1a, L.7.1c, SL.7.1)
    - Clip editorials or other examples of writing from newspapers or magazines to use to look for phrases and clauses.
- Homework and Practice—In class discussions, explain the function of phrases and clauses in general. Create T-charts to identify phrases and clauses in a variety of sentences by listing the clauses on one side of the chart and phrases on the other. Discuss what you notice about the items on the T-chart. (L.7.1a, SL.7.1)
    - Check out the text *Teaching Grammar with Perfect Poems for Middle School* by Nancy Mack (2008).
- Homework and Practice—Add and edit phrases and clauses in a variety of sentence types to argumentative, informative/explanatory, narrative and other types of writing as needed. (L.7.1a, L.7.1b, L.7.1c, W.7.1, W.7.2, W.7.3, W.7.10, WHST.7.1, WHST.7.2, WHST.7.10)
- Cooperative Learning—Do a Kagan Cooperative Learning structure called Think-Pair-Share.[1] With a partner, practice writing, sharing, and comparing sentences that include simple, compound,

complex, and compound-complex. Partners decide on the type (declarative, interrogative, imperative, exclamatory) and form (simple, compound, complex, and compound-complex) of the sentence to practice. Each partner thinks about a sentence and then writes it down. Partners share their sentences and each checks the other's for accuracy. Pairs may also underline clauses and circle phrases. If both agree, raise hands to show the teacher. If sentence is correct, partners repeat the process with a different type and form of sentence. (L.7.1b, L.7.1c, SL.7.1)

- Homework and Practice—Clip editorials or other examples of writing from newspapers or magazines and edit for sentence structures. Identify examples of as many different forms as possible. Attach clippings to posters to illustrate various structures and post for all to see. Rewrite sentences to correct misplaced and dangling modifiers. (L.7.1b, L.7.1c)
- Homework and Practice—Do a sentence "walkabout." The teacher will post chart papers labeled "Simple," "Compound," "Complex" and "Compound-Complex." At the end of daily reading assignments or at different times throughout the week, students reflect on the topics or skills being learned and write a sentence to reflect the topic or a skill in the form indicated on the chart. Students walkabout until they have written a sentence of each kind. The teacher will read the sentences at the beginning of the next class to review previous learning. If there are mistakes in the sentence structure, use that time also to correct the mistakes. (L.7.1b, SL.7.1)
- Homework and Practice—Identify and use various forms of capitalization, punctuation, and spelling when writing. (L.7.2)
    - Edit and correct your writing for capitalization errors.
    - Edit and correct your writing for punctuation errors, including the use of commas in coordinate adjectives.
    - Edit and correct your writing for spelling errors.
- Homework and Practice—Create flashcards to practice spelling words. (L.7.2)
- Homework and Practice—Use and edit for commas in coordinate adjectives, a series, introducing a speaker, or in clauses. (L.7.2, W.7.1, W.7.2, W.7.3, W.7.10, WHST.7.1, WHST.7.2, WHST.7.10)
- Homework and Practice—Select precise words to reflect your intent in speaking and writing and when describing what authors are trying to say. (L.7.3)
- Nonlinguistic Representations—Create a symbol or draw an image or picture to help you remember the meaning of a word. (L.7.4)
- Homework and Practice—Create a word wall for the class to use or individual card files for students to use. Write new words, noting

affixes, roots, parts of speech, and the meaning as it is used in context. Note whether the word is of Greek or Latin origin. (L.7.4)
- Homework and Practice—Create a chart on the wall to identify words with Greek or Latin affixes and roots. Add to the chart as you identify new words. The chart should have columns for prefixes, suffixes, roots, and root definition, origin, and examples. Add new words to the column for examples. Your teacher may provide specific affixes and roots to look for, but some common ones are listed below. (L.7.4b)

> Prefixes: anti, bell, dif, dis, epi, eu, ex, fore, inter, intra, intro, macro, micro, peri, pseudo, re, semi, super, un
> Suffixes: ation, cian, ed, eous, es, ic, ical, ing, ition, ly, ness, ous, s, ure
> Roots: cide, corp, cred, demos, dorm, ec, eco, frater, gen, liber, logy, mar, mater, meter, mono, mut, omni, pater, phyt, poly, proto, scope, ver, zoa

- Homework and Practice—Use general and specialized print and digital reference materials to determine word pronunciation or determine or clarify its precise meaning or its part of speech. (L.7.4c)
- Homework and Practice—Create a wall chart or class spreadsheet for literary, biblical, mythological, and historical allusions. The chart should include columns for the allusion, to whom or what it alludes, and the meaning of the allusion. Interpret the allusions below and add to the chart. You may need to do a little research to interpret the allusions. (L.7.5a, SL.7.1)

  - Literary Allusions—

    A nose like Pinocchio's.
    He acted like a Scrooge.
    He is such a Romeo with the ladies.
    Chocolate was her Achilles' heel.
    Divine Comedy by Dante Alighieri

  - Biblical Allusions—

    She was a good Samaritan for helping them.
    What a Garden of Eden this place is!
    You couldn't be more of a Solomon!
    The lava ate the forest like Jonah.
    A fly in the ointment
    Cast the first stone
    Doubting Thomas
    I don't know him from Adam!
    Man does not live by bread alone.
    The love of money is the root of all evil.

The blind leading the blind

- Mythological Allusions —

  Cupid
  Herculean
  Nemesis
  Pandora's box
  Promethean

- Historical Allusions —

  Attila the Hun
  Berserk
  Casanova
  Chauvinist
  Machiavellian
  Marathon

- Homework and Practice — As a class, use the various sources listed to locate and/or identify allusions and interpret their meanings. Identify the line, paragraph, or page number and add to the wall chart of allusions. (L.7.5a, SL.7.1)

  - Poetry and Songs —

    "A Little East of Jordan" by Emily Dickinson
    "Ah, Sun-flower" by William Blake
    "Bright Star, Would I Were Steadfast as Thou Art" by John Keats
    "Bronzes" by Carl Sandburg
    "Does Anybody Hear Her?" by Casting Crowns
    "Judas" by Lady Gaga
    "Love Story" by Taylor Swift
    "Robin Hood" by John Keats
    "Standing Tall" by Jamie McKenzie
    "That Don't Impress Me Much" by Shania Twain
    "The Divine Image" by William Blake
    "The Three Enemies" by Christina Rossetti
    "The Magi" by William Butler Yeats
    "The Wasteland" by T. S. Eliot
    "Turn! Turn! Turn!" by The Byrds

  - Literature —

    Hamlet by William Shakespeare
    The Iliad by Homer
    The Odyssey by Homer
    The Wednesday Wars by Gary D. Schmidt (2009)

- Picture Books That Teach Allusion (kimscorner4teachertalk.com)

    Goldilocks Returns by Lisa Campbell Ernst (2003)
    Hey, Mama Goose by Jane Breskin Zalben (2005)
    John, Paul, George and Ben by Lane Smith (2006)
    Tar Beach by Faith Ringgold (1996)
    Where is the Green Sheep by Mem Fox (2010)
    Wild About Books by Judy Sierra (2004)

- Commercials and Websites—

    Adam and Eve (2005) (http://commercial-archive.com/node/12574)
    David and Goliath (1995) (http://commercial-archive.com/node/9074)
    Moses (2005) (http://commercial-archive.com/node/12367)
    Noah (2002) (http://commercial-archive.com/node/1959)
    Noah's Ark (2001) (http://commercial-archive.com/node/4433)
    http://examples.yourdictionary.com
    http://mythologyteacher.com/documents/biblical_allusions.pdf
    www.buzzle.com/articles/allusion-examples.html
    www.infoplease.com/ipa/A0934910.html

- Homework and Practice—When defining words, write a sentence using an antonym or a synonym of the word you are defining. Write a sentence to describe how the meaning of the original sentence changed when you used the synonym or the antonym. (L.7.5b)
- Homework and Practice—Create lists of analogies to understand the relationship between words. As you read, identify examples of word relationships. You can create a chart or other graphic organizer to illustrate the relationships of cause/effect, part to whole, and item to category. Discuss the relationships and how the analogy explains the relationship. (L.7.5)

    - Cause/Effect—
        - Tornado is to destruction as drought is to famine.
        - Earthquake is to tsunami as heavy rain is to flood.
    - Part to Whole—
        - Petal is to flower as pages are to a book.
        - Leaves are to trees as bricks are to a house.

- Item to Category—
    - Oaks are to trees as rings are to jewelry.
    - Apples are to fruits as Monopoly is to games.
- Take Notes—As you read in all subject areas, add new words to general academic and domain-specific vocabulary card files, journals, or class spreadsheets. Use new words and phrases where appropriate to expand written and spoken English. (L.7.6)
    - You could also create vocabulary notebooks that also contain a picture that describes the term and definition so it will be easier for you to remember both.

NOTE

1. Kagan, S., & Kagan, M. (1997). *Kagan Cooperative Learning Smart Card* (pp. 2–3). San Clemente, CA: Kagan Publishing.

NINE
Grade 7 Strategies and Activities for Reading Literacy in History and Social Studies

Choose literary or informational text from Grades 6–8 text exemplars selections or other appropriate grade-level selections. Grade 6–8 exemplars are noted with an (EX). You may also select primary sources from the sites listed below. The standards are grade-span in nature, but the text suggestions and activities are on a Grade 7 level.

PRIMARY SOURCES WEBSITES

(www.lib.berkeley.edu/instruct/guides/primarysourcesontheweb.html)

- Ad*Access   http://scriptorium.lib.duke.edu:80/adaccess/—advertisements from the United States and Canada from 1911 to 1955
- American Civil War Homepage, http://sunsite.utk.edu/civil-war—images, documents, and photographs from the Civil War
- American Memory, http://lcweb2.loc.gov/ammem/—digitized collections of documents, moving pictures and text, photographs, sound
- American Studies Web, www.georgetown.edu/crossroads/asw/archives.html—general American history resources
- Bancroft Library, http://bancroft.berkeley.edu/collections/—contains a wide variety of special collections
- Documenting the American South, http://docsouth.unc.edu—Southern literature, slave narratives, first-person narratives

- Edsitement, http://edsitement.neh.gov/websites.html?all—history, language arts, and social studies sites maintained by the National Endowment for the Humanities
- Euro Docs, http://eudocs.lib.byu.edu/—historical documents from western Europe*
- HarpWeek, http://app.harpweek.com/—Harper's Weekly from 1857 to 1865
- Historical Newspapers Online, http://historynews.chadwyck.com/—various newspaper articles from 1790 to 1980
- History Matters, http://historymatters.gmu.edu/—first-person narratives of average Americans
- Internet Library of Early Journals, http://ww.bodley.ox.ac.uk/ilej/—eighteenth- and nineteenth-century journals
- Primary Sources at Yale, www.yale.edu/collections_collaborative/primarysources/tools.html
- U.S. Historical Documents Online, http://w3.one.net/%7Emweiler/ushda/list.htm—historical documents from the time of Columbus through the Civil Rights Act of 1991
- Valley of the Shadow: Living the Civil War in Pennsylvania and Virginia, http://jefferson.village.virginia.edu/vshadow/vshadow.html—lists of additional websites for studying the Civil War
- World War II Resources, www.ibiblio.org/pha

STRATEGIES AND ACTIVITIES

- Compare and Contrast—In class discussions on how to cite a primary or secondary source, create an example of APA, Chicago, MLA, or other formats your teacher wants you to use. Check with the Library of Congress website to follow their guidelines for citing online historical archives. Create a graphic organizer to illustrate the differences or create samples of each. Discuss how each is similar and different. Keep the examples for future reference in your journals or posted on the wall in the classroom. (RLHS.6-8.1)
- Take Notes—As you read, take notes of bibliographic information for future reference. Include a citation of each text used and a summary of the information used from the text. (RLHS.6-8.1)
- Homework and Practice—As you analyze sources to determine whether they are primary or secondary, cite specific textual evidence to support analysis. Refer to appendix E to help analyze documents for primary sources. (RLHS.6-8.1)
- Compare and Contrast—Create a list of primary and secondary sources for a research topic. Check the primary sources websites to help create your lists. In class discussion, analyze how the two types of sources are the same, how they are different, the kinds of

information each source provides, and state the benefits of each source. (RLHS.6-8.2)
- Summarize—Read a variety of primary and secondary sources for your topic to determine the central ideas of or information in the source. Write accurate summaries of primary and secondary sources distinct from prior knowledge or opinions. (RLHS.6-8.2, WHST.6-8.10)
- Take Notes—Read through primary or secondary sources and take notes on specific details found in the documents to help determine central ideas or information. Include citations in your notes so you do not have to look them up again. Follow the format given to you by your teacher. Remember that primary sources include birth certificates, business receipts, court records, diaries, firsthand newspaper accounts, journals, letters, maps, photos, or transcripts of interviews or speeches. Secondary sources include biographies, book and movie reviews, encyclopedias, essays, news articles, public television documentaries, and social studies texts. (RLHS.6-8.2)
- Cooperative Learning—To break up large quantities of text to determine central ideas and information found in primary and secondary sources, get students into groups of four or more to do a Kagan Cooperative Learning structure called Jigsaw.[1] Divide students into groups and give each group a chunk of information. That group reads, discusses, and answers questions on the information to become "experts." When each group "knows" their information, they then divide into other groups to share their portion of what each learned. (RLHS.6-8.2, SL.7.1)
  - For example: give each student a colored chip or slip of paper. Ask them to get into groups so that the group is made up of different colors with no duplicate colors. Students will then get into groups of the same color, such as all blues together, reds together, etc. You will need to decide the numbers of colors and groups prior to grouping. Hand out the chunked material to be learned. When students are ready, direct them to get back into their original group and have them share their information. You will also need to direct the order of the sharing when using colors.
    - You can also create groups using playing cards aces through ten. Hand out your chunks accordingly so that the first part goes to the aces, the second goes to the deuces, the third to the threes, and so on. This makes sharing in the group much easier.
    - Students will summarize the information to give to the original group.

- Homework and Practice—Read a variety of texts to identify key steps in a text's description of a process related to history/social studies. Create a graphic organizer such as a content web or timeline or flowchart to illustrate the steps. Have students share their processes with the class. (RLHS.6-8.3, RLHS.6-8.10, SL.7.1, SL.7.6)

  - How to become a U.S. citizen

    How to Become a US Citizen 6th Edition: A Step-By-Step Guidebook for Self Instruction by Sally Navarro (2001)

  - How to become an FBI agent

    How to Become an FBI Agent by William Thomas (2009)

  - How a bill becomes law

    From Inspiration to Legislation: How an Idea Becomes a Bill by Amy Black (2006)

    Easy Simulations: How a Bill Becomes a Law: A Complete Toolkit with Background Information, Primary Sources and More by Pat Luce and Holly Joyner (2008)

  - How to register to vote

    http://registertovote.org

  - How to open a checking account

    www.ehow.com/how_2814_open-bank-account.html
    Everything Kids' Money Book by Brette McWhorter Sember (2008)

  - How to run for public office

    How to Become an Elected Official by Mike Bonner (2000)
    How to Run for Political Office and Win by Melanie Williamson (2011)
    Running for Public Office by Sarah De Capua (2002)

  - How to be a leader in student government

    The Essential Student Government Guide by Eric Williams (2008)

  - How to become an entrepreneur

    How to Run a Lemonade Stand by Russell Cope (2013)
    How to Become an Entrepreneurial Kid by Dianne Linderman (2011)

  - How to build your own country

    How to Build Your Own Country by Valerie Wyatt (2009)

Strategies and Activities for Reading Literacy in History and Social Studies 115

- Questions—So students can gain a deeper understanding of words and phrases in context, create a game of "Ask Me Three." Students should define the words and phrases first. The teacher then asks three questions related to the words or phrases, and the student or small groups of students respond. You might wish to let students create the questions to strengthen their ability to ask higher order questions. (RLHS.6-8.4)

    - How would you describe the relationship to/between ____ and ____?
    - How is ____ related to ____?
    - What would be a good example of ____?
    - Which clues from context helped you to understand the meaning of the word/phrase?
    - How would you classify ____?

- Homework and Practice—Have students create term and definition flashcards or add terms and definitions to their vocabulary notebooks or card files. (RLHS.6-8.4)

    - Create word search puzzles where students identify the terms based on the definition or short definitions based on the terms.
    - Create Vocabulary Bingo cards with terms in the Bingo squares. Teacher calls out a definition and students mark the square, attempting to make a "bingo."
    - If definitions are or can be made brief, use definitions in the bingo squares and call out the terms (www.ehow.com/list_6120736_middle-school-vocabulary-activities.html).
    - Create *Jeopardy!* game questions based on the terms and definitions. Use the term in the *Jeopardy!* squares and have students ask the question based on the definition.

- Homework and Practice—Create a concept web. In each circle of the web, write one vocabulary word or phrase related to your topic. Branching off from each circle will be the definition of the word or phrase and additional information to show how it is related to the topic. (RLHS.6-8.4)

- Compare and Contrast—Create a three-circle Venn diagram to compare and contrast signal words that illustrate how a text presents information in nonfiction text written sequentially, comparatively, and causally. Share your diagram with a partner and compare. Locate several signal words in a text you are currently reading to determine how information is presented in it. Will you always have words to indicate sequential order? (RLHS.6-8.5)

- Compare and Contrast—Identify texts on the same topic that present information differently (sequentially, comparatively, cau-

sally). Write an essay to compare and contrast one text structure to another text structure with regard to the information presented. (RLHS.6-8.5)
- Nonlinguistic Representations—Draw pictures to represent a sequence of events, comparison or cause and effect relationship in a historical event. (RLHS.6-8.5)
- Nonlinguistic Representations—Create comic strip frames of five to eight sections to illustrate a historical event found in your current classroom social studies or history text. Cut the frames apart and let a partner sequence the events. Signal words may or may not be included. (RLHS.6-8.5)
- Nonlinguistic Representations—Create historical event timelines using illustrations or symbols. (RLHS.6-8.5)
- Questions—Use stem statements to help develop questions when working with information presented in texts. (RLHS.6-8.5)
  - Sequential Questions—
    - What events or steps are listed?
    - Are there substages and if so, what are they?
    - Is the order of events important?
    - Can the order be changed and not affect the event?
    - What happens if the order of events is changed?
    - What is the time span of events?
    - What is being explained by the events?
  - Comparative Questions—
    - What is being compared?
    - How are the events or people alike?
    - How are they different?
    - What are the qualities of each item?
    - How do they correspond to one another?
  - Causal Questions—
    - What happened first?
    - What happened as a result?
    - What might happen next?
    - Why did the event happen?
    - How did the event happen?
    - How did people react to the event or consequences of the event?
- Homework and Practice—Use the following texts or other grade-appropriate texts to practice determining informational text structure. This list was compiled by Carol Brooks Simoneau, EdD. (RLHS.6-8.5)

- Sequential—

    The Amazing Life of Benjamin Franklin by James Cross Giblin (2000)
    Ice Cream by William Jasperson (1988)
    Sugaring Time by Kathryn Lasky (1983)
    Castle by David Macaulay (1977)
    The Buck Stops Here by Alice Provensen (1990)
    My Place by Nadia Wheatley (1992)

- Comparative—

    Merry Ever After: The Story of Two Medieval Weddings by Joe Lasker (1977)
    Outside and Inside Trees by Sandra Markle (1993)
    The Inside-Outside Book of Washington, D.C. by Roxy Munro (2001)
    The Great Fire by Jim Murphy (2010)
    People by Peter Spier (1988)

- Causal—

    Why Mosquitoes Buzz in People's Ears by Verna Aardema (1992)
    Conestoga Wagons by R Ammon (2000)
    If You Give a Mouse a Cookie by Laura Joffe Numeroff (2010)
    The Old Red Rocking Chair by Phyllis Root (1992)
    Nettie's Trip South by Ann Turner (1995)
    A New Coat for Anna by Harriet Ziefert (1988)

- Homework and Practice—Conduct a scavenger hunt for examples of text written in sequential, comparative or causal format. Search textbooks, newspapers, magazines, journals and other nonfiction texts in your classroom and/or library. Jot down the name and page number of the texts. Which format did you find the most examples of? Can you explain why? (RLHS.6-8.5)
- Homework and Practice—Collect several copies of the comics from the daily and weekend newspapers. Cut the comics into separate frames, putting each comic into an envelope. Direct students to look at the frames and put into sequential order. How do you know you have the correct order? Work individually or with a partner. (RLHS.6-8.5, SL.7.1)
- Homework and Practice—As a daily or weekly activity, write one part of a cause/effect sentence on the board. Write the cause and let students suggest reasonable effects, or write the effect and ask for reasonable causes. (RLHS.6-8.5)
- Homework and Practice—Look outside the classroom for cause and effect relationships. As you see them, jot them down and share

with a partner or the class. Be able to state the cause and the effect. (RLHS.6-8.5)

- A woman donated Civil War photos to the museum to complete their collection.
- The candidate received 55 percent of the vote so he won the election.

- Homework and Practice—Create storyboards to illustrate sequences of events. (RLHS.6-8.5)
- Questions—To help determine an author's purpose or point of view of a primary source, consider a variety of questions. Look at a primary source with a partner and try to answer the questions to help you determine purpose or point of view. (RLHS.6-8.6, SL.7.1)

  - Was the text handwritten, published, or printed?
  - What type and quality of paper was used? You may have to do some additional research to determine this.
  - What type of font was used if it was published?
  - Are there special images, pictures, or borders on the document?
  - How is the information arranged?
  - Does the text appear to be a personal letter or a document that was meant to persuade?
  - For whom was the document created?

- Homework and Practice—Look at a variety of advertisements throughout history to help determine author's purpose and point of view. Advertisements are good resources to use to look for loaded language as well as inclusion or avoidance of particular facts. Use the website for Ad*Access. http://scriptorium.lib.duke.edu:80/adaccess. Create a class chart to help you determine purpose and point of view. The chart should have columns for the name of the ad, loaded words, inclusion of facts, and avoidance of facts. Each student should analyze an ad, complete the chart based on information from the ad, create a statement of author's purpose and/or point of view, and then share the chart and statement with a partner or the class. (RLHS.6-8.6, SL.7.1)
- Nonlinguistic Representations—Individually or in small groups, students create tables, charts, graphs, models or diagrams to represent quantitative or technical information presented in words found in science or technical subjects text. Student share representations with the class. (RLHS.6-8.7, SL.7.1)

  - Add tables, charts, graphs, models or diagrams, to individual or group presentations.

- Take Notes—Create a class table or chart with four columns—one each for the name of the source (newspaper, magazine, editorial, letter to the editor, journal article, or textbook selection), Facts, Opinions, and Reasoned Judgments. As a class, look at various sources to determine the facts, opinions, and reasoned judgments. Be able to justify how you classified the statement. Make selections from those listed or other grade-appropriate text. Please check sources for appropriateness prior to classroom use. (RLHS.6-8.8, SL.7.1)

  American Girl
  Discovery Girls
  Girl's Life
  Junior Scholastic Grades 6–8 for social studies and current events
  National Geographic for Kids
  Sports Illustrated for Kids
  www.dogonews.com
  www.gogonews.com
  www.headlinespot.com/for/kids
  www.newspaperforkids.com
  www.teachingkidsnews.com
  www.timeforkids.com

- Take Notes—Analyze the relationship between a primary and secondary source on the same topic. Choose a topic of interest. Check the web for primary sources on your topic. Identify three primary sources and locate actual or copies of the sources. Then identify and locate three secondary sources. Research each and take notes as to specific information found in each. Jot down a citation for the information you find so you can refer to it later. Describe in class discussion how the primary sources are related to the secondary sources with regard to the types and reliability of information found in each. (RLHS.6-8.9, RLHS.6-8.1, SL.7.1)
- Take Notes—As a class, create a chart to list information from primary and secondary sources for a specific topic. Analyze the relationship between the two sources by identifying how the items in each list are similar and different. What kind of information is found with each type? Use the primary source worksheet in appendix E. Use the chart to compare and contrast the items on each list. Write a class conclusion to state the benefits of using primary and secondary sources. (RLHS.6-8.9, SL.7.1)
    - Primary sources include birth certificates, census records, court records, diaries, first hand newspaper accounts, journals, letters, photographs, receipts, transcripts of interviews or speeches, etc.

- Secondary sources include biographies, book or movie reviews, encyclopedia entries, essays, newspaper articles, public television documentaries, social studies texts, etc.

- Hypothesize and Test—Research a historical event of interest. With a partner or in a small group, create a hypothesis based on the event and use primary and secondary sources to support or contradict your hypothesis. Cite all sources. Present your hypothesis and findings to the class. (RLHS.6-8.9, RLHS.6-8.1, SL.6.1)
- Questions—When considering primary and secondary sources on the same topic, ask to answer a variety of questions. (RLHS.6-8.9)
  - Was the author of the document present at the event? If so, how long after the event was the information recorded?
  - When was the secondary source written?
  - Do the secondary sources or other primary sources support or contradict the information?
  - Did the author of either the primary or secondary source have reasons to be honest or dishonest?
  - Who are the intended audiences of the sources?
  - What is the importance of the secondary source?
  - Is there a connection between the authors of the two sources? If so, what? If not, what is the interest of the secondary author?
  - Why was the secondary source written?
  - What questions are raised after you analyze the primary and the secondary sources?

- Hypothesize and Test—Think about various documents and texts from history. Generate and test hypotheses based on historical documents. For example, think about the Bill of Rights. You could hypothesize that there are ten amendments that comprise the Bill of Rights. What would happen if one or two of the amendments were removed from the Bill of Rights? Write a hypothesis and test it. You may need to do some research to determine the outcome. (RLHS.6-8.10)
- Homework and Practice—Read a variety of history and social studies texts. Some could include those listed below. (RLHS.6-8.10)

    A good history/social studies resource to use to address a variety of CCSS reading and writing standards is www.historysimulation.com. Here you will find a variety of interactive activities for Civil War, World War I, World War II, and Cold War instruction.
    A History of US: War, Peace, and All That Jazz by Joy Hakim (EX)
    A Young Patriot: The American Revolution as Experienced by One Boy by Jim Murphy (1998)

Cathedral: The Story of Its Construction by David Macaulay (EX)
Duel: The Parallel Lives of Alexander Hamilton and Aaron Burr by Judith St. George (2009)
5000 Miles to Freedom: Ellen and William Craft's Flight from Slavery by Ellen and William Craft (2006)
George Washington: Frontier Colonel by Sterling North (2006)
Ghost Soldiers: The Epic Account of World War II's Greatest Rescue Mission by Hampton Sides (2002)
How Would You Survive in the Middle Ages by Fiona MacDonald (1997)
Never to Forget: The Jews of the Holocaust by Milton Meltzer (1991)
Outrageous Women of the Middle Ages by Vicki Leon (1998)
She Touched the World by Sally Hobart Alexander (2008)
The Boys' War: Confederate and Union Soldiers Talk about the Civil War by Jim Murphy (1993)
The Horrible, Miserable Middle Ages: The Disgusting Details about Life during Medieval Times by Kathy Allen (2010)
The Medieval World by Philip Steele (2006)
The Secret of the Priest's Grotto by Peter Lane Taylor (2007)
The True Stories of D-Day by Henry Brook (2006)
Truce: The Day the Soldiers Stopped Fighting by Jim Murphy (2009)

NOTE

1. Kagan, S., & Kagan, M. (1997). *Kagan Cooperative Learning Smart Card* (pp. 2–3). San Clemente, CA: Kagan Publishing.

TEN
Grade 7 Strategies and Activities for Reading Literacy in Science and Technical Subjects

Choose literary or informational text from Grades 6–8 text exemplars selections or other appropriate grade level selections. Grades 6–8 exemplars are noted with an (EX). The standards are grade-span in nature, but the text suggestions below and activities are on a Grade 7 level.

SCIENCE AND TECHNOLOGY TEXTS

A Life in the Wild: George Schaller's Struggle to Save the Last Great Beasts by Pamela S. Turner (2008)

Almost Astronauts: 13 Women Who Dared to Dream by Tanya Lee Stone (2009)

An American Plague: The True and Terrifying Story of the Yellow Fever Epidemic of 1793 by Jim Murphy (2003)

Bodies from the Ice: Melting Glaciers and the Recovery of the Past by James Deem (2008)

Cars on Mars: Roving the Red Planet by Alexandra Siy (2011)

Chew on This: Everything You Don't Want to Know about Fast Food by Eric Schlosser (2007)

Guinea Pig Scientists: Bold Self-Experimenters in Science and Medicine by Mel Boring (2005)

How They Croaked: The Awful Ends of the Awfully Famous by Georgia Bragg (2012)

In Your Face: The Culture of Beauty and You by Shary Graydon (2004)

Little People and a Lost World: An Anthropological Mystery by Linda Goldenberg (2006)

Mr. Lincoln's High-Tech War by Thomas B. Allen (2009)

Phineas Gage: A Gruesome but True Story about Brain Science by John Fleischman (2004)

Secret of the Yellow Death: A True Story of Medical Sleuthing by Suzanne Jurmain (2013)

Shark Life: True Stories about Sharks and the Sea by Peter Benchley (2007)

The Hive Detectives: Chronicle of a Honey Bee Catastrophe by Loree Griffin Burns (2013)

The Pluto Files: The Rise and Fall of America's Favorite Planet by Neil DeGrasse Tyson (2009)

The Telephone Gambit: Chasing Alexander Graham Bell's Secret by Seth Shulman (2009)

The Wright Sister: Katherine Wright and Her Famous Brothers by Richard Mauer (2003)

Tracking Trash: Flotsam, Jetsam, and the Science of Ocean Motion by Loree Griffin Burns (1999)

Up Close: Rachel Carson by Ellen Levine (2008)

Written in Bone: Buried Lives of Jamestown and Colonial Maryland by Sally Walker (2009)

STRATEGIES AND ACTIVITIES

- Compare and Contrast—In class discussions on how to cite a source, create an example of APA, Chicago, MLA, or another format your teacher wants you to use. Create a graphic organizer to illustrate the differences or create samples of each. Discuss how each is similar and different. Keep the examples for future reference in your journals or posted on the wall in the classroom. (RLST.6-8.1)
- Take Notes—As you read, take notes of bibliographic information for future reference. Include a citation of the text used and a summary of the information used from the text. (RLST.6-8.1)
- Compare and Contrast—Compare and contrast conclusions in texts on the same topic. Create a Venn diagram or other appropriate graphic organizer to illustrate same and different conclusions. Share the organizer with a partner and discuss why the conclusions may or may not differ. (RLST.6-8.2, SL.7.1)
- Summarize—Write accurate summaries of texts distinct from prior knowledge or opinions. Summaries may be shared with the class. (RLST.6-8.2, WHST.6-8.2, SL.7.1)
- Cooperative Learning—To break up large quantities of text to determine central ideas and information, get students into groups of four or more to do a Kagan Cooperative Learning structure called Jigsaw.[1] Divide students into groups and give each group a chunk of information. That group reads, discusses, and answers questions

on the information to become "experts." When each group "knows" their information, they then divide into other groups to share their portion of what each learned. (RLST.6-8.2, SL.7.1, SL.7.6)

- For example, give each student a colored chip or slip of paper. Ask them to get into groups so that the group is made up of different colors with no duplicate colors. Students will then get into groups of the same color, such as all blues together, reds together, and so on. You will need to decide the numbers of colors and groups prior to grouping. Hand out the chunked material to be learned. When students are ready, direct them to get back into their original group and have them share their information. You will also need to direct the order of the sharing when using colors.
- You can also create groups using playing cards aces through ten. Hand out your chunks accordingly so that the first part goes to the aces, the second goes to the deuces, the third to the threes, and so on. This makes sharing in the group much easier.
- Students will summarize the information to give to the original group.

- Nonlinguistic Representations—Create drawings on posters to illustrate central ideas of a text. (RLST.6-8.2)
    - Create a model, mobile, or diorama to show central ideas or conclusions.

- Homework and Practice—Read a variety of texts based on science and technical topics. Determine the central ideas or conclusions of a text. Jot down the title and author of the text and state the ideas and conclusions in a reading journal. Cite evidence to support your analysis. (RLST.6-8.2, RLST.6-8.1)
- Compare and Contrast—Compare and contrast multistep procedures when carrying out experiments. Choose a topic such as how to make tin can ice cream. Locate a recipe on the Internet to describe the procedures. Write out the steps on one side of a T-chart. Find another recipe similar to the first one and write those steps out on the other side of the T-chart. Consider the directions, temperatures, measurements, etc. Write an essay that details the similarities and differences. Consider why there are differences in the recipes with regard to procedures and measurements and state your conclusion in your essay. Introduce and develop your topic with relevant facts and concrete details. Use appropriate transitions and precise language. Edit your writing for grammar and mechanics. (RLST.6-8.3, WHST.6-8.2)

- Other topics include making pudding (instant and cooked), rock candy, soap bubble shapes, volcanoes; poke a stick or needle through a balloon. Check science experiment resources for other topics.
- Nonlinguistic Representations—Design a series of drawings or diagrams to illustrate a multistep procedure prior to carrying out experiments. (RLST.6-8.3)
- Homework and Practice—Read a variety of science and technical subject texts. Choose and follow a multistep procedure to carry out experiments, take measurements, or perform technical tasks. Choose procedures from the texts listed or other grade-appropriate texts. (RLST.6-8.3, RLST.6-8.10)

   Crime-Solving Science Projects: Forensic Science Experiments by Kenneth Rainis (2005)
   Draw 50 Buildings and Other Structures: The Step-By-Step Way to Draw Castles and Cathedrals, Skyscrapers and Bridges, and So Much More . . . by Lee J. Ames (2013)
   Help! I'm Teaching Middle School Science by C. Jill Swango and Sally Bowles Steward (2002)
   Information Literacy and Technology Research Projects: Grades 6–9 by Norma Heller (2001)
   Power Point for Teachers: Dynamic Presentations and Interactive Classroom Projects (K–12) by Ellen Finkelstein and Pavel Samsonov (2007)
   Science Experiments You Can Eat (Revised Edition) by Vicki Cobb (1984)
   Science Methods Investigation: A Step-by-Step Guide for School Students by Schyrlet Cameron, Carolyn Craig, and Sherryl Soutec (2010)
   Science Sleuths: Solving Mysteries Using Scientific Inquiry by Howard Schindler (2009)
   Sewing School: 21 Sewing Projects Kids Will Love to Make by Andria Lisle and Amie Plumley (2010)
   Steven Caney's Ultimate Building Book by Steven Caney (2006)
   Summer Bridge Activities, Grades 6–7 by Frankie Long, Leland Graham, and Katie Fields (1998)
   The Art of Construction: Projects and Principles for Beginning Engineers and Architects by Mario Salvadori (2000)
   32 Quick and Fun Content Area Comprehension Activities for Middle School by Lynn Van Gorp (2006)

- Homework and Practice—Conduct research on how-to topics of interest. Work in small groups to develop a project and demonstrate multistep procedures to the class. Prepare a graphic organizer to illustrate your steps. Write an explanatory narrative on the procedures, experiments, or technical processes used. Introduce and develop your topic with relevant, well-chosen facts, definitions, concrete details, or other information and examples. Use appropriate transitions, precise language, and domain-specific vocabulary. (RLST.6-8.3, WHST.6-8.2, SL.7.1. SL.7.6)

- Design a class webpage with text images and hyperlinks.
- Create a webpage for a significant person from social studies, science, or a technology inventor.
- Create a class blog.
- Add animation to presentations.
- Produce a commercial using Movie Maker.
- Create a travel documentary using PowerPoint.
- Plan and produce a podcast.

- Homework and Practice—Add new words and phrases to a vocabulary journal or card file. Check words for affixes and roots and determine whether the word is Greek or Latin in origin. Discuss with a partner what you think the word means; then use print or digital resources to define the word. Is there a synonym or antonym? Use a thesaurus to check for both. Write a sentence using the new word in your journal or card file. Add an illustration or diagram to help remember the word. (RLST.6-8.4)
- Homework and Practice—Create flashcards with terms on one side and definitions as the word is used in context to the other. (RLST.6-8.4)
- Homework and Practice—Create crossword puzzles with terms and definitions. Share the puzzles with a partner or as a class activity. (RLST.6-8.4)
- Homework and Practice—Create a question of the day related to symbols, terms, and domain-specific words and phrases. Post questions on the board adding new questions each day. For example: What is the definition of ____? Does the word remind you of another term? How is it related to ____? What would be the opposite of ____? Where would you find an example of ____? (RLST.6-8.4)
- Homework and Practice—Create a class classification chart and add words and phrases as they are learned so students begin to have a better understanding of the different sciences. Create columns for "Life Science," "Physical Science," "Earth Science," "Scientific Inquiry," and "Technology." If the word or phrase fits in more than one column, add it and discuss why it would be acceptable to list in all that apply. (RLST.6-8.4, SL.7.1)
- Compare and Contrast—Authors of science and technical subject textbooks generally organize texts in a specific manor appropriate to the content. Authors will structure texts in formats of compare

and contrast, cause and effect, sequence, problem and solutions, and description. Many times authors will use multiple structures. Compare and contrast a narrative text to a science or technical subject text in an essay. Create a Venn diagram first to determine how the texts are similar and different. Use the organizer to write your essay. Introduce and develop your topic with relevant, well-chosen facts, definitions, concrete details, or other information and examples. Use appropriate transitions, precise language, and domain-specific vocabulary. Edit your writing for grammar and mechanics. (RLST.6-8.5, WHST.6-8.2, L.7.1b–c, L.7.2, L.7.3)

- Compare and Contrast—Read selections representative of author's purposes to explain something, describe a procedure, and discuss an experiment. Write an essay that compares and contrasts the topics and why the authors chose to write the selections in the manner in which they were written. Introduce and develop your topic with relevant, well-chosen facts, definitions, concrete details, or other information and examples. Use appropriate transitions, precise language, and domain-specific vocabulary. Cite textual evidence where necessary. Edit your writing for grammar and mechanics. (RLST.6-8.5, RLST.6-8.1, WHST.6-8.2, L.7.1b–c, L.7.2, L.7.3)
- Compare and Contrast—Conduct research on a topic of interest, researching reading texts, experiments (where applicable), simulations, videos, and multimedia sources on the same topic. Take notes, remembering to add citations to the notes as you go for future reference. Create a graphic organizer to organize your thoughts. Share your organizer with a partner and your presentation plan. Consider the suggestions of your peers. Compare and contrast the information from your reading text to two other sources. How is the information alike? Different? What did you learn from each source you didn't learn from the other sources? Is there a difference in the way the information was presented in each source? Do all sources present facts and reasoned judgments or do any sources present opinions? Write an essay to share your findings. Introduce and develop your topic with relevant, well-chosen facts, definitions, concrete details, or other information and examples. Use appropriate transitions, precise language, and domain-specific vocabulary. Edit your writing for grammar and mechanics. (RLST.6-8.5, RLST.6-8.1, WHST.6-8.2, L.7.1b–c, L.7.2, L.7.3)

  - Suggested Resources (always check websites prior to use)—

    Mysteries of Antiquity: Lessons to Engage Middle School Students in Ancient/Medieval History by Max Fischer (2001)
    Short Role-Playing Simulations for Middle School World History by Richard Di Giacomo (2012)
    www.americaslibrary.gov—Learn about America's story

www.archives.gov/research—Research the National Archives for photos and documents

www.brighthubeducation.com/middle-school-history-lessons/110630-europe-in-the-middle-ages-teaching-ideas—Middle school students learn about life in Medieval Europe

www.csun.edu/~hcedu013/onlineactivities.html—Online simulation activities

www.ebscohost.com/public/science-reference-center—Simulations, videos, and more

www.kidzsearch.com—Safe, family-friendly search engine for kids

www.middleschool.net/curlink/science/scimain.htm—Middle school science activities

http://msms.ehe.ous.edu/tag/simulations—Quality resources for math and science simulations

www.nationalparkservice.org—Research the National Park Service to find out information on monuments and other information about the states

www.techtrekers.com/webquests/social.html—Social studies and science simulations

- Summaries—Write summaries of texts for each type of structure. (RLST.6-8.5, WHST.6-8.2)
- Nonlinguistic Representations—Read a science or technical subject text. Create an illustrated diagram, concept web, or other graphic organizer to show how the major sections of the text contribute to the whole and the understanding of the topic. Share and discuss the organizers with the class. (RLST.6-8.5, SL.7.1)
  - Draw a series of pictures or create a timeline with pictures to illustrate sequences.
- Cooperative Learning—Consider texts where authors use multiple structures. In groups of four, read a selection or text, noting structure signal words. Create a group table with headings that include title of the text, compare and contrast, cause and effect, sequence, problem and solution, and description. As you read, write down the signal words in the appropriate columns and the page numbers where the words were found for quick reference. Discuss in your group which structure was used most and why the author chose to use more than one structure. Does it help or hinder your comprehension? The group should formulate an answer, write it down, and be prepared to share it with the class. (RLST.6-8.5, SL.7.1, SL.7.6)

- Check out the list of texts at http://emilykissner.blogspot.com that details texts and specific text structures. Multiple structure texts include

  Face to Face with Dolphins by Flip Nicklin (2007)
  Frogs: Strange and Wonderful by Laurence Pringle (2012)
  Leo the Snow Leopard by Craig Hatkoff (2010)
  Saving the Ghost of the Mountain by Sy Montgomery (2009)
  The Secret Life of a Snowflake by Kenneth Libbrecht (2010)

- Cooperative Learning—Divide the class into teams and scavenger hunt for specific examples of text structure in classroom texts. Students should look through magazines, newspapers, textbooks, and nonfiction books. There should be enough resources for students to locate at least one example of each text structure. Teams can then create a graphic organizer to illustrate each example they found. Teams can then present their organizers to the class. (RLST.6-8.5, SL.7.1)
- Questions—When analyzing the structure used by an author, there are many questions you can ask to help deepen the meaning of the text. (RLST.6-8.5)
  - Comparison and Contrast—
    - What did the author use in the comparison?
    - Were analogies used and how?
    - What are the similarities and differences?
    - Why did the author compare ____ to ____?
    - What signal words designate the organization as comparison and contrast?
    - What are the major sections of the text?
    - How do the sections contribute to the whole of the text or selection?
    - How do the sections help you understand the topic?
    - What questions do you still have?
    - Why do you think the author chose this organizational format?
  - Cause and Effect—
    - What event is described?
    - What are the causes discussed?
    - What are the effects discussed?
    - How did you make the distinction between the cause(s) and the effect(s)?
    - What are the major sections of the text?
    - How do the sections contribute to the whole of the text or selection?

- How do the sections help you understand the topic?
- What questions do you still have?
- Why do you think the author chose this organizational format?

- Sequence—
  - What event is sequenced?
  - What are three to five events the author shared?
  - What is the main event in the sequence? How do you know?
  - What words or phrases were used to show sequence?
  - What are the major sections of the text?
  - How do the sections contribute to the whole of the text or selection?
  - How do the sections help you understand the topic?
  - What questions do you still have?
  - Why do you think the author chose this organizational format?

- Problem and Solution—
  - What is the problem?
  - What statement(s) from the selection explain(s) the problem?
  - What is the solution presented by the author?
  - What other solutions might the author have presented?
  - What are the major sections of the text?
  - How do the sections contribute to the whole of the text or selection?
  - How do the sections help you understand the topic?
  - What questions do you still have?
  - Why do you think the author chose this organizational format?

- Description—
  - What does the author describe? What images do you "see" in your mind's eye?
  - What are the characteristics of the ____ that the author shared?
  - What other characteristics would you share about the ____?
  - Which signal words helped you to identify the selection as description?
  - What are the major sections of the text?
  - How do the sections contribute to the whole of the text or selection?

- How do the sections help you understand the topic?
- What questions do you still have?
- Why do you think the author chose this organizational format?

• Homework and Practice—Check out the list of texts at http://emily-kissner.blogspot.com that details texts and specific text structures. Some of these texts may be at younger levels but are still useful to teach the structures. (RLST.6-8.5)

- Compare and Contrast—

    Are You a Snail? by Judy Allen (2003)
    Butterfly or Moth? How Do You Know? by Melissa Stewart (2011)
    Frog or Toad? How Do You Know? by Melissa Stewart (2011)
    Nathan of Yesteryear and Michael of Today by Brian Heinz (2006)
    Shark or Dolphin? How Do You Know? by Melissa Stewart (2011)
    What's the Difference between an Alligator and a Crocodile by Lisa Bullard (2010)
    What's the Difference between a Leopard and a Cheetah? by Lisa Bullard (2009)

- Cause and Effect—

    Energy Makes Things Happen by Kimberly Bradley (2002)
    Extreme Animals by Nicola Davies (2006)
    Just the Right Size: Why Big Animals Are Big . . . by Nicola Davies (2009)
    Living Sunlight: How Plants Bring the Earth Life by Molly Bang (2009)
    Mysterious Messages by Gary Blackwood (2009)
    Unsolved History: Enigmatic Events by Gary Blackwood (2005)

- Sequence—

    A House Spider's Life by John Himmelman (2000)
    A Puffin's Year by Katherine Zecca (2007)
    The Amazing Impossible Erie Canal by Cheryl Harness (1999)
    Flute's Journey by Lynne Cherry (1997)
    Looking at Glass through the Ages by Bruce Koscielniak (2006)
    Owen and Mzee: The Language of Friendship by Isabella Hatkoff (2007)

Trapped by the Ice: Shakelton's Amazing Antarctic Adventure by Michael McCurdy (2002)

- Problem and Solution —

    A Place for Birds by Melissa Stewart (2009)
    A Place for Butterflies by Melissa Stewart (2006)
    Falcons Nest on Skyscrapers by Priscilla Jenkins (1996)
    The Secret of the Yellow Death by Suzanne Jurmain (2009)
    Sparrow Jack by Mordicai Gerstein (2003)
    When the Wolves Returned by Dorothy Hinshaw Patent (2008)

- Description (these texts are from a list compiled by Carol Brooks Simoneau, EdD) —

    A Dragon in the Sky by Laurence Pringle (2001)
    Crocodiles and Alligators by Seymour Simon (2001)
    Feathers by Dorothy Patent (1992)
    It Could Still Be a Bird by Allan Fowler (1990)
    Safari Beneath the Sea by Diane Swanson (1994)
    What the Moon Is Like by Franklyn Branley (1986)

- Homework and Practice — Create and post a class list of signal words for each structure — comparison and contrast, cause and effect, sequence, problems and solutions, and description. Scan current texts and trade books or others provided to begin your list. Add to the list as you read. There are several words you can add. As words are added to the list, write sample sentences for each structure and discuss in class how each new sentence fits the structure. (RLST.6-8.5, SL.7.1)

    - Compare and Contrast —
        - Similar
        - Different
        - Either/or
        - Compared to
        - However
        - In contrast

    - Cause and Effect —
        - Because
        - As a result of
        - If/then
        - Since
        - Therefore
        - Due to

- Sequence—
  - First, second, etc.
  - Next
  - Before
  - Finally
  - During
- Problem and Solution—
  - Possible answer
  - A problem is
  - A solution is
  - Is solved by
- Description—
  - The characteristics are
  - For example
  - For instance
  - Contains
  - To illustrate

- Homework and Practice—Create and share graphic organizers to illustrate each type of structure. Use a short nonfiction text to help create your graphic organizer. Create story maps for multiple structure texts, Venn diagrams for compare and contrast, cause and effect organizers, problem-solution frames, and tables or charts for descriptions. (RLST.6-8.5)
- Homework and Practice—Use advance organizers to introduce new content, analyze the organizational structure, and aid in understanding of the topic (see appendix G). (RLST.6-8.5)
- Homework and Practice—Use SQRRR before a new chapter or unit of content (see appendix A). (RLST.6-8.5)
- Homework and Practice—Read an article or other selection that provides an explanation. Discuss the article with a partner. Write an essay to describe what is explained, what new information was learned, how you can use the information, and identify any new questions you now have. Who would benefit most from the explanation? Does the author try to convince or persuade you about something connected to the explanation? Explain your reasoning and cite textual evidence when necessary. Introduce and develop your topic with relevant, well-chosen facts, definitions, concrete details, or other information and examples. Use appropriate transitions, precise language, and domain-specific vocabulary. Edit your writing for grammar and mechanics. (RLST.6-8.5, RLST.6-8.1, WHST.6-8.2, L.7.1b–c, L.7.2, L.7.3)

- Create a graphic organizer to answer the questions and share it with a partner prior to writing the essay.
- Homework and Practice—Read an article or other selection that describes a procedure. Discuss it with a partner. Write an essay to describe the focus of the procedure itself and what the author is trying to explain. Why does the author feel the need to describe the procedure? Who would benefit most from the description? Is the author's explanation of the procedure clear, or do you have new questions? Explain your reasoning and cite textual evidence when necessary. Introduce and develop your topic with relevant, well-chosen facts, definitions, concrete details, or other information and examples. Use appropriate transitions, precise language, and domain-specific vocabulary. Edit your writing for grammar and mechanics. (RLST.6-8.5, RLST.6-8.1, WHST.6-8.2, L.7.1b–c, L.7.2, L.7.3)
- Homework and Practice—Read an article or other selection that describes or discusses an experiment. Discuss it with a partner. Write an essay to identify the focus of the experiment and the author's reason for describing or discussing it. What is the author trying to teach you? How can you use the new information? Who would benefit most from the description of the experiment? What new questions do you have? Introduce and develop your topic with relevant, well-chosen facts, definitions, concrete details, or other information and examples. Use appropriate transitions, precise language, and domain-specific vocabulary. Explain your reasoning and cite textual evidence when necessary. Edit writing for grammar and mechanics. (RLST.6-8.5, RLST.6-8.1, WHST.6-8.2, L.7.1b–c, L.7.2, L.7.3)
- Compare and Contrast—Before students can determine author's purpose to explain or describe procedures or experiments, they should know the differences and components of each. In small groups create a three-circle Venn diagram to illustrate the similarities and differences in explanations, procedures and experiments. Groups should then share their findings with each other and misconceptions should be corrected. (RLST.6-8.6, SL.7.1)
- Summaries—Read a nonfiction selection and write a summary of the author's explanation, description of a procedure, or discussion of an experiment. (RLST.6-8.6, WHST.6-8.2)
- Compare and Contrast—Choose two technical texts on the same or similar topics. Create a graphic organizer to illustrate the similarities and differences in the quantitative or technical information presented in words and visuals. Share your organizer with the group or class. (RLST.6-8.7, RLST.6-8.10, SL.7.1)

- Select from texts such as—

  13 Buildings Children Should Know by Annette Roeder (2009)
  Amazing Buildings by Philip Wilkinson (1993)
  Brooklyn Bridge by Lynn Curlee (2001)
  Cathedral: The Story of Its Construction by David Macaulay (2013)
  City: A Story of Roman Planning and Construction by David Macaulay (1983)
  From Mud Huts to Skyscrapers by Christine Paxmann (2012)
  How to Read Churches: A Crash Course in Ecclesiastical Architecture by Denis McNamara (2011)

- Take Notes—Read a technical text and take notes on a graphic organizer. What information did you learn from the quantitative or technical words and what did you learn from the information expressed visually? Which helped most—the words or the visuals? Discuss your organizers and answer the question in class discussion. (RLST.6-8.7, RLST.6-8.10, SL.7.1)
- Nonlinguistic Representations—Individually or in small groups, students create tables, charts, graphs, models, or diagrams to represent quantitative or technical information presented in words found in science or technical subjects text. Students share representations with the class. (RLST.6-8.7, SL.7.1)

  - Add tables, charts, graphs, models, or diagrams to individual or group presentations.

- Take Notes—Create a class table or chart with four columns—one each for the name of the source (newspaper, magazine, editorial, letter to the editor, journal article, or textbook selection), "Facts," "Opinions," and "Reasoned Judgments." As a class, look at various sources to determine the facts, opinions and reasoned judgments. Be able to justify how you classified the statement. Make selections from those listed or other grade-appropriate text. Please check sources for appropriateness prior to classroom use. (RLHS.6-8.8, SL.7.1)

  www.dogonews.com/category/science
  http://eurekalert.org/kidsnews
  http://info@nanooze.org
  http://kids.nationalgeographickids.com/kids/stories
  www.odysseymagazine.com
  www.sciencecastle.com/sc/index.php/home/science_news
  www.sciencenews.org
  www.student.societyforscience.org

http://teacher.scholastic.com/activities/scholasticnews
www.timeforkids.com/news-archive/science

- Nonlinguistic Presentations—Create a model, diorama, display, collage, or scrapbook to represent information gained from reading texts, experiments, simulations, videos, and multimedia sources on the same topic. (RLST.6-8.9, RLST.6-8.10)

NOTE

1. Kagan, S., & Kagan, M. (1997). *Kagan Cooperative Learning Smart Card* (pp. 2–3). San Clemente, CA: Kagan Publishing.

ELEVEN

Grade 7 Strategies and Activities for Writing in History, Social Studies, Science and Technical Subjects

Choose literary or informational text from Grades 6–8 text exemplars selections or other appropriate grade level selections. Grades 6–8 text exemplars are noted with an (EX). The standards are grade-span in nature, but the text suggestions and activities are on a Grade 7 level.

- Homework and Practice—Write an argument to criticize a resource you used in researching a topic; offer two to three ways to improve the resource. Support the claims with reasoned logic. Be specific as to how and why the resource was worthy of criticism. Did you find incorrect data? Did the author have appropriate knowledge of the topic? Draw and cite evidence from informational texts to support your analysis and research. Introduce and support claims with relevant, accurate data and evidence; distinguish claims from alternate or opposing claims; and use words, phrases and clauses to create cohesion. Write and edit the argument for grammar and mechanics. Prepare to share the argument with the class. (WHST.6-8.1, WHST.6-8.4, WHST.6-8.5, WHST.6-8.8, WHST.6-8.9, WHST.6-8.10, RI.7.1, SL.7.1, L.7.1b-c, L.7.2, L.7.3)
- Homework and Practice—Write a variety of arguments on discipline-specific content distinguishing the claims from alternate or opposing claims, using organized reasons and evidence. Support your claim(s) with logical reasoning and relevant, accurate data and evidence. Use appropriate words, phrases, and clauses for cohesion. Maintain a formal style and provide a concluding statement. Draw and cite evidence from informational texts to support your analysis and research. Introduce and support claims with rele-

vant, accurate data and evidence; distinguish claims from alternate or opposing claims; and use words, phrases and clauses to create cohesion. Edit your argument for grammar and mechanic. You may be asked to present your argument to the class. (WHST.6-8.1, WHST.6-8.4, WHST.6-8.5, WHST.6-8.6, WHST.6-8.8, WHST.6-8.9, WHST.6-8.10, RI.7.1, SL.7.1, L.7.1b–c, L.7.2, L.7.3)

- Topic suggestions—
    - Choose any war and debate an issue from that war.
    - Choose any president and debate a particular policy of the administration.
    - The death penalty should/should not be banned in America.
    - The U.S. government should/should not invest more time and money in alternative sources of energy.
    - China is/is not a threat to America's supremacy.
    - Outsourcing jobs has/has not led to unemployment in America.
    - Guantanamo prison should/should not be closed by the U.S. authorities.
    - The United States does/does not have a responsibility to support human rights initiatives in other countries.
    - Global warming is/is not a fact.
    - Christmas break/songs/activities/trees should/should not be renamed "holiday."
    - The driving age in the United States should/should not be raised to eighteen.
    - Driving licenses for high school students should/should not be tied to grades.
    - The United States should/should not continue to act as a peacekeeper to the world.
    - Washington, D.C., should/should not be the fifty-first state.
    - Military recruiting in schools does/does not invade student privacy.
    - Nonlegal students should/should not be allowed to attend college.
    - Nonlegal students should/should not be allowed to attend college on out-of-state tuition.
    - The United States should/should not increase space exploration.
    - Civilians should/should not be allowed to carry weapons.
    - The United States should/should not increase its use of nuclear power.

- The United States should/should not increase its production of oil.
- Schools should/should not use standardized testing.
- High school students should/should not have to pass a national exit exam to graduate.
- Supreme Court proceedings should/should not be televised.
- Professional athletes should/should not be allowed to compete in Olympic Games.
- Students should/should not say the Pledge of Allegiance each day in school.
- The United States should/should not devote more time and money to building a space station on the moon.

- Compare and Contrast—Consider arguments or informative or explanatory presentations and your topic. Compare and contrast some aspect of your topic with that of another presentation on a similar topic in an essay. What is similar and different? Create an outline to organize your thoughts. Draw and cite evidence from informational texts to support your analysis and research. Seek guidance and support from peers and adults. Write and edit your essay for grammar and mechanics. Use appropriate words, phrases, and clauses for cohesion. Maintain a formal style and provide a concluding statement. Use technology to produce and publish your writing. (WHST.6-8.2, WHST.6-8.4, WHST.6-8.5, WHST.6-8.6, WHST.6-8.9, WHST.6-8.10, RI.7.1, SL.7.1, SL.7.6, L.7.1b-c, L.7.2, L.7.3)
- Compare and Contrast—Choose two historical advertisements for similar products. You can choose from Ad*Access or other appropriate sources. Write an essay to compare and contrast the two ads. What was the author's purpose and how do you know? Based on the loaded words, which product would you buy and why? Did the author succeed in her purpose? Use appropriate words, phrases, and clauses for cohesion. Maintain a formal style and provide a concluding statement. Draw and cite evidence from informational texts to support analysis. Edit your paper for grammar and mechanics. (WHST.6-8.2, WHST.6-8.4, WHST.6-8.5, WHST.6-8.6, WHST.6-8.9, RI.7.1, L.7.1b-c, L.7.2, L.7.3)
- Homework and Practice—Conduct research to learn about a scientist, inventor, historical personality, or someone you've read about in a technical subject. Pretend you are that person and you are going to be interviewed for a newspaper from your time period. What would you want to be asked and how would you respond? Draw and cite evidence from informational texts to support your analysis and research. Write a narrative interview based on infor-

mative texts using transitions, precise language, and formal style. Share your "interviews" with the class. Edit for grammar and mechanics. (WHST.6-8.2, WHST.6-8.4, WHST.6-8.6, WHST.6-8.8, WHST.6-8.9, WHST.6-8.10, RI.7.1, SL.7.1, L.7.1b–c, L.7.2, L.7.3)

- Possible topics—
  - Famous World War I or World War II heroes
  - Famous generals of the Civil War
  - Famous leaders of the Revolutionary War
  - The first person to reach the North Pole
  - Hannibal
  - Julius Caesar
  - Constantine
  - Ramses II
  - Augustus
  - Albert Einstein
  - George Washington Carver
  - Marie Curie
  - Sir Isaac Newton
  - George Simon Ohm
  - Anders Celsius
  - John Dalton
  - Henry Bell
  - Samuel Morse
  - John Venn
  - Elias Howe
  - Louis Pasteur
- Homework and Practice—Conduct research using multiple print and digital sources on a topic related to a technical subject and write an informative or explanatory report or develop a project. Your teacher will give you specific criteria to follow. Develop your topic with relevant, well-chosen facts, definitions, concrete details, quotations, or other information. Use appropriate transitions, precise language, and domain-specific vocabulary in a formal style and objective tone. Choose from topics listed or other appropriate topics. Include quantitative or technical information in the form of a visual as well as a model, diorama, or other product that represents something about your topic. Draw and cite evidence from informational texts to support your analysis and research. Edit your writing for grammar and mechanics. Use technology to produce and publish your writing. Share your report or project with the class. (WHST.6-8.2, WHST.6-8.4, WHST.6-8.5, WHST.6-8.6, WHST.6-8.8, WHST.6-8.9, WHST.6-8.10, RI.7.1, SL.7.1, L.7.1b-c, L.7.2, L.7.3)

- Topic suggestions—
    - How do computers work?
    - How do computer viruses work?
    - What are technical requirements for making medicines?
    - What is cloud printing?
    - What is artificial intelligence?
    - How does GPS work and where is it used?
    - What is computer architecture and how does it work?
    - What technologies are available to homeowners to help conserve energy?
    - What are the current trends in technology products people buy today?
    - How have televisions changed in the last twenty-five years?
    - What is data mining?
    - Why is it necessary to guard personal information and not put it on the Internet?
    - How is communication affected by social media?
    - What is cyber security and why is there a need for it?
    - Where does spam come from and how can we stop it?
    - How does a search engine work?
- Homework and Practice—Conduct research using multiple print and digital sources on a topic related to a science or technical career and write an informative or explanatory report. Your teacher will give you specific criteria to follow. Develop your topic with relevant, well-chosen facts, definitions, concrete details, quotations, or other information. Use appropriate transitions, precise language, and domain-specific vocabulary in a formal style and objective tone. Choose from topics listed or other appropriate topics. Address the career prep courses, job description, day to day duties, salary or pay, and where in the country or world the career opportunities are the best. What is one interesting fact that you would not associate with your topic? Include quantitative or technical information in the form of a visual as well as a model, diorama, or other product that represents something about your topic. Edit your writing for grammar and mechanics. Use technology to produce and publish your writing. Share your report or project with the class. (WHST.6-8.2, WHST.6-8.4, WHST.6-8.5, WHST.6-8.6, WHST.6-8.8, WHST.6-8.9, WHST.6-8.10, RI.7.1, SL.7.1, L.7.1b–c, L.7.2, L.7.3)
    - Database administrators
    - Network engineers
    - Software engineers
    - Computer analyst

- Mechanical engineer
- IT manager
- Web programmer
- Civil engineer
- Storm chasers
- Biological scientist
- Clinical lab technicians
- Clinical lab technologists
- Geoscientists and hydrologists
- Environmental scientists
- Biochemists
- Medical scientists
- Atmospheric scientists
- Physicists
- Material scientists
- Astronomers
    - As a postwriting activity, complete a "I think I'd like to be a . . ." T-chart that lists the pros and cons for the career you chose. Share the chart with a partner or the class after your presentation.
    - If possible, interview and/or job shadow someone in the career field you chose to gain personal insight to that career.
- Homework and Practice—Conduct research using multiple print and digital sources on a topic related to history and social studies and write an informative or explanatory report. Your teacher will give you specific criteria to follow. Develop your topic with relevant, well-chosen facts, definitions, concrete details, quotations, or other information. Use appropriate transitions, precise language, and domain-specific vocabulary in a formal style and objective tone. Choose from topics listed or other appropriate topics. Include a model, diorama, illustration, or other product that represents something about your topic. Draw and cite evidence from informational texts to support your research. Edit your writing for grammar and mechanics. Use technology to produce and publish your writing. Share your report or project with the class. (WHST.6-8.2, WHST.6-8.4, WHST.6-8.5, WHST.6-8.6, WHST.6-8.8, WHST.6-8.9, WHST.6-8.10, RI.7.1, SL.7.1, L.7.1b–c, L.7.2, L.7.3)
    - Topic suggestions—
        - What is the history of comic books?
        - What is the history of your hometown?
        - What historical events happened on your birthday?

- What are the craziest laws still on the books in your town?
- What happened during the Salem Witch trials?
- What are the five most important cultural events in the last century? How and why are they important?
- Many inventions came from the Middle Ages and the Renaissance and are still important today. Choose one invention and identify the inventor and analyze the invention's effect on life from the time of the invention up through today.
  - Wheelbarrow
  - Yo-yo
  - Horse collar
  - Water thermometer
  - Adding machines
  - Wallpaper
  - Scales for weighing
  - Oil painting
  - First parachutes
  - Bell chimes
  - Submarine
  - Pencil
  - Telescope
  - Bit and bridle
  - Heavy plough
  - Hourglass
  - Blast furnace
  - Spinning wheel
  - Quarantine
- Homework and Practice—Conduct research using multiple print and digital sources on a topic related to science and write an informative or explanatory report. Your teacher will give you specific criteria to follow. Develop your topic with relevant, well-chosen facts, definitions, concrete details, quotations, or other information. Use appropriate transitions, precise language, and domain-specific vocabulary in a formal style and objective tone. Choose from topics listed or other appropriate topics. Include a model, diorama, illustration, or other product that represents something about your topic. Draw and cite evidence from informational text to support your research. Edit your writing for grammar and mechanics. Use technology to produce and publish your writing. Share your report or project with the class. (WHST.6-8.2, WHST.6-8.4, WHST.6-8.5, WHST.6-8.6, WHST.6-8.8, WHST.6-8.9, WHST.6-8.10, RI.7.1, SL.7.1, L.7.1b–c, L.7.2, L.7.3)

- Topic suggestions—
    - How and why did some species of animals become extinct while others did not?
    - How does nuclear power work?
    - Select a simple machine and write an explanation about how it works.
    - How does music affect one's mood?
    - Choose two insects and describe the differences and how each adapted to its environment.
    - Describe an experiment to be conducted on a space shuttle.
    - What are the latest discoveries in astronomy?
    - If the world stopped spinning, what is the last thing you would see and hear?
    - Do electric toothbrushes remove more plaque than manual toothbrushes?
    - Arch bridge, beam bridge, and suspension bridge: which bridge will support more weight?
    - How effective are air furnace filters?
    - How does temperature affect mold growth?
    - Do incandescent bulbs produce more heat than fluorescent bulbs?
    - How does climate dictate lifestyle?
    - How does weather affect your mood?
    - What is the most important mineral and why?
    - What causes volcanic eruptions and when and where were the deadliest volcanic eruptions?
    - Identify and describe the functions of the basic equipment in your science lab.
    - What is the relationship between heat absorption and color?
    - What are the best materials for insulation?
    - How does salt affect rusting?
    - How does background noise affect our concentration?
    - How does music influence learning and memory?
    - How does temperature affect water density?
    - What is animation and how is it done?
    - How and what do antioxidants do?
    - How does music affect plant and animal behavior?
    - Does shoe design affect an athlete's jumping height?
    - What are the risks of artificial tanning?
    - What causes tornadoes?

- Homework and Practice—Select a paragraph or larger selection written in one organizational structure and rewrite it in another organizational structure. What changes did you have to make with regard to the information? What other changes did you have to make? (WHST.6-8.2, RLHS.6-8.5, RLST.6-8.5)
- Summaries—After selecting a topic and conducting initial research, write summaries about what you would most like to learn or know about the topic. (WHST.6-8.7)
- Take Notes—Identify sources for research and write down the bibliographic information for use later. (WHST.6-8.7)
- Hypothesize and Test—Create a hypothesis worksheet (see appendix D). Complete the worksheet to help you focus on your topic and develop your hypothesis. (WHST.6-8.7)
- Questions—When you begin research, consider a variety of questions. (WHST.6-8.7)

    - What are five to ten questions you most would like to answer about your topic?
    - What are three to five specific sources you can use to learn about your topic and why?
    - What are five to ten ways you can share information about your topic?
    - How would you divide your topics into subtopics?
    - Is there someone you can interview and what questions would you ask?

- Questions—When conducting research, ask and find answers to a variety of relevant questions based on stem statements in appendix C. (WHST.6-8.7)
- Homework and Practice—Conduct short research projects to answer questions using a variety of sources and generating additional focused questions that allow for continued exploration. Choose from the following topics or others supplied by your teacher. Consider questions you would most like to answer through your research on a topic. Choose one question and conduct research to answer that question. Present your question and answer in the form of a press conference or news story to the class. End your presentation with additional questions that inspire continued exploration of the topic. (WHST.6-8.7, WHST.6-8.2, WHST.6-8.4, WHST.6-8.5, WHST.6-8.6, WHST.6-8.8, WHST.6-8.10, SL.7.1, L.7.1b-c, L.7.2, L.7.3)

    - Topic suggestions—
        - How has technology changed in the past fifty years? One hundred years?
        - What does technology mean to you?

- What are the benefits to studying a foreign language?
- Which national monument or symbol of America do you think best represents America and why?
- What career would you dislike the most and why?
- How does science affect eating habits, shopping patterns, and sports activities?
- What is the most important mineral and why?
- How does the geography of where you live affect the culture?
- How did trains and railroads change life in America?
- How is bulletproof clothing made?
- What Olympic events were practiced in Ancient Greece?
- How has the music industry been affected by the Internet and digital downloading?
- How does texting affect literacy?
- How are black holes formed?
- How is Internet censorship used in China and around the world?
- What is the history of—
    - Video games
    - Lasers
    - Donut holes
    - Potato chips
    - Chocolate chip cookies
    - Silly putty
    - Velcro
    - Popsicles
    - Cheese
    - Teflon
    - Nylon
    - Cereal
    - Slinky

- Homework and Practice—Practice writing hypothesis questions and "If/then" statements. See appendix D for a sample. (WHST.6-8.7)

Appendix A: Summary Frames

Narrative Frame
1. Who are the main characters and what are they like?
2. Where and when does the story take place?
3. What prompted the action in the story?
4. How did the characters express their feelings?
5. What did the main characters decide to do? If they set a goal, what was it?
6. How did the main characters try to accomplish their goal?
7. What were the consequences?

Definition Frame
1. What is being defined?
2. To which general category does the item belong?
3. What characteristics separate the item from other things in the general category?
4. What are some different types or classes or the item being defined?

Problem-Solution Frame
1. What is the problem?
2. What is a possible solution?
3. What is another possible solution?
4. Which solution has the best chance of succeeding?

Argumentation Frame
1. What information is presented that leads to a claim?
2. What is the basic statement or claim that is the focus of the information
3. What examples or explanations are presented to support this claim?
4. What concessions are made about the claim?

Somebody-Wanted-But-So-Then Frame

Somebody: identify the character
Wanted: state the goal of the character
But: state the problem/conflict
So then: state the resolution

SQRRR Frame

> Survey: Read and record the main titles and subtitles from the chapter sections
> Question: Turn topic headings into questions—who, what, where, when, why and how
> Read: Read the text to answer the questions you just asked, taking notes as you go
> Recite: Answer the questions you asked orally and in your own words
> Review: Write a short summary that answers each question you asked

Bio-Poem

> Line 1: Person's first name
> Line 2: Four adjectives that describe the person
> Line 3: Likes (name three things) example: Likes dogs, cats, turtles
> Line 4: Gives (name three things) example: Gives hope, comfort, kisses
> Line 5: Fears (name three things) example: Fears strangers, new places, photographers
> Line 6: Would like to see (name three things) example: Would like to see Paris, Atlanta, tigers
> Line 7: Who lives (name the city or place)
> Line 8: Person's last name

Appendix B: Position Paper Format

Introductory Paragraph— State your thesis or argument (this is your view of the issue) Introduce the topic Use organized structure	This paper will argue that . . . (thesis)
Premise 1— Give a single concept, idea, body of evidence Include facts, evidence and support Include your own analysis and interpretation	(Restate your thesis) because . . .
Premise 2— Give a single concept, idea, body of evidence Include facts, evidence and support Include your own analysis and interpretation	(Restate your thesis) because . . .
Premise 3— Give a single concept, idea, body of evidence Include facts, evidence and support Include your own analysis and interpretation	(Restate your thesis) because . . .
Concluding Paragraph— Restate your thesis Restate each premise Give no new information *(You can begin your conclusion with words such as finally, in a word, in brief, in conclusion, in the end, in the final analysis, on the whole, thus, to conclude, to summarize, in sum, in summary)	In conclusion*, (thesis). First, because (premise 1). Second, because (premise 2). Third, because (premise 3).

Appendix C: Stem Questions

Post these stem questions and statements with your Verbs to Question list. Refer to both in classroom instruction as you work toward implementing higher order questions in classroom instruction.

- Can you make a distinction between . . . ?
- Can you recall, name, select, list . . . ?
- Compare two like characters, people, events, places, causes-effects.
- Could you explain your reasons?
- Define _____ using context clues.
- Describe the relationship between _____ and _____ .
- Do you agree with the actions or outcome . . . ?
- Explain how . . .
- Explain the meaning of . . .
- Explain which clues from the text helped you understand the meaning.
- Give an example of . . .
- How did the title of _____ give a clue to the action/event that followed?
- How does _____? Support your answer.
- How does _____ compare/contrast with _____ ?
- How is _____ related to _____ ?
- How would you classify, compare, contrast . . . ?
- How would things be different if . . . ?
- Identify the characteristics of . . .
- List _____ major events in order.
- List the differences/similarities in . . .
- Show or explain the role of . . .
- What examples can you find . . . ?
- What facts or ideas show . . . ?
- What ideas can you add to . . . ?
- What criteria might you use to judge or evaluate . . . ?
- What evidence supports . . . ?
- What is your opinion of . . . ?
- What are the characteristics of . . . ?
- What approach or strategy could you use to . . . ?
- What could happen if . . . ?
- What might be the result of . . . ?

- What might you infer from . . . ?
- What conclusions might be drawn from . . . ?
- What ideas or details can you add to . . . ?
- What was the most important event . . . ?
- What would be an example . . . ?
- What would be the benefit(s) of . . . ?
- Who, what, when, where, why . . . ?
- Why do you think . . . ?
- Why was the setting important . . . ?

Appendix D: Hypothesis Worksheet

State your topic.
 The topic I am researching is:

Write the question.
 The question I want to answer is:

State what you already know about the topic.
 I know these three things about my topic:

 1.
 2.
 3.

Conduct research using various sources to find important information about your topic—
 New information on my topic includes:

The hypothesis is_____.
 What will the answer to your question be? Make a prediction in the form of an if/then statement.

Appendix E: Primary Source Analysis

Directions: Analyze and evaluate primary documents and record your information here. You may not use all questions for all documents.

Title:

Date of the document:

General subject in the document:

Type of document:

Who created the document?

Who was the intended audience?

Why was the document written?

What is the author's point of view?

What specific examples of bias do you find?

How is the author connected to the document?

Is there a similar document that confirms or contradicts information in this primary source?

What is it and what information is confirmed or contradicted?

What are two new things you learned?

Look up and define any new terms or phrases.

What does the document help you to see about life or the culture of the time?

What new questions do you have now?

Appendix F: SMART Goals

S = Specific: Be specific about what you want to accomplish—who will be involved, where will it take place, what exactly needs to be done?

M = Measurable: How will you know you have accomplished your goal?

A = Attainable: Is the goal within reach—not too easy or too difficult?

R = Relevant: Is the goal worth accomplishing at this time?

T= Timely: What is the deadline to reach the goal?

Appendix G: Sample Grade 7 Advance Organizers

Create advance organizers for new stories, dramas, poems, or new informational text and share with students prior to reading.
Use graphic organizers like

- KWL charts
- Flowcharts
- Outlines
- Webs
- SQRRR strategies

- 5W and How
- Timelines
- Narrative frames
- Venn diagrams

Use expository advance organizers to describe the new content to be learned. Here is an example:

Today we begin to read about the Mayflower Pilgrims, who traveled to the new world in 1620, as we read the book Rush Revere and the Brave Pilgrims *by Rush Limbaugh (2013).*

As we read, we will determine the theme and central ideas of the text, and in class discussions we will look at how the ideas are conveyed through the use of details. You will individually create a graphic organizer to illustrate the development of the theme or central idea over the course of the text, and as a class, we will analyze how specific elements of the story interact with characters or the plot.

We will discuss the text structure and how it contributes to its meaning. You will also want to cite several pieces of textual evidence to support your analysis of what the text says and infers. We will also look at length at the charts, graphs, photos, and other visual information in the text to get a sense of what life was really like, and will look at photos, paintings, illustrations, and drawings of people who were there.

Finally, you will write an informative/explanatory essay to describe how an author develops and contrasts the points of view of different characters or narrators in the text. You will introduce and develop your topic using relevant facts, definitions, details, and quotations. Use appropriate transitions and precise language and a concluding statement. Cite several pieces of textual evidence to support your analysis. Edit your essay for grammar and mechanics. (RL.7.1, RL.7.2, RL.7.3, RL.7.6, W.7.2, W.7.4, W.7.5, W.7.9, W.7.10, SL.7.1, SL.7.6, L.7.1b–c, L.7.2, L.7.3, RLST.6-8.7)

A narrative advance organizer could look like this:

I remember a past vacation my family took when I was in seventh grade. We went back East to visit some relatives in Plymouth, Massachusetts. I didn't think I would enjoy the trip because of all the work I would have to do.

My teacher knew we were going visit the Pilgrim Hall Museum, and she had an idea about what I would see there. For my assignment, I had to read a couple of documents on display there, and I had to figure out the theme and central ideas of each document and describe how the ideas were conveyed through the use of details. I had to give her several details and even cite the documents I read.

Then she had me create a graphic organizer to show how the theme and central ideas were developed in the documents. I found several brochures with great pictures and photos and was able to cut them up and use them on my organizer.

There was so much to see in the museum: charts, graphs, maps, photos, memorabilia, old tools, and other items—I really had a feeling for what life was like for the people who lived there hundreds of years ago. My last assignment was to write an informative/explanatory essay to describe what life must have been like for someone my age. I had to introduce and develop my topic using relevant facts, definitions, details, and quotations. I also had to use appropriate transitions, precise language and a concluding statement. I had to figure out how to cite several pieces of evidence by calling the town librarian because I had never used documents or exhibits like those before. I wrote and edited my essay for grammar and mechanics, and my aunt let me use her computer to type it.

My teacher was pretty impressed with my homework, and you know what? I was impressed with how much I learned and how much fun I had doing it. (RL.7.1, RL.7.2, RL.7.10, W.7.10, L.7.1b–c, L.7.2, L.7.3, RLST.6-8.7)

To practice skimming, use the book *William Bradford: Plymouth's Faithful Pilgrim* by Gary D. Schmidt (1998). Use the information to create an outline or a concept web.

Appendix H: Sample Parent Letter

Date:

Dear Parent or Guardian:
    Today we worked on the following skills or concepts in class:

1.
2.
3.

Please let your son or daughter share with you the above skills or concepts as he or she practices them at home. As you share this time with your child, it would be helpful if you would look for the following as your child practices:

Your child and I appreciate your time as you help him or her achieve success through practice.

Sincerely,

Appendix I: Products and Performances

The following list of products and performances gives you suggestions for alternative homework assignments, projects, or performance assessments. You will find activities to address a wide range of grade levels and student abilities suitable for the implementation of CCSS.

Acrostic poems	Directions
Advertisements	Displays
Art product	Dramatizations
Artifact analysis	Drawings
Attribute chart	Essays
Audio tape	Experiment
Autobiography	Eyewitness report
Banner	Fable
Board games	Fairy tale
Book cover	Family tree
Bookmark	Film critique
Brochure	Flags
Bulletin board	Flowchart
Captions	Foods
Cartoons	Forum on an issue
CD covers	Game
Characterizations	Glossary
Character study	Graph
Chart	Greeting card
Choral reading	Haiku
Clay sculpture	Illustrated story
Collage	Illustrations
Collections	Interview
Creative writings	Invitation
Crosswords	Journals
Demonstrations	Learning center
Diagrams	Letter to the editor
Diary	Letter—personal
Dictionary	Logo
Diorama	Logs (reading)

Lyrics
Magazine articles
Map
Mind map
Mobile
Model
Montage
Mosaic
Movie clip
Mural
Museum exhibit
News report
Newsletter
Note cards
Oral presentations
Outline
Painting
Pamphlet
Panel discussion
Pantomime
Papier-mache
Paraphrase
Pen-pal project
Photo album
Photo essay
Picture story
Plan
Play
Poetry
Poetry anthology
Poll
Portfolio
Position paper
Poster
Pottery
Presentation
Press conference
Project cube
Prototype
Puppet
Puppet show
Puzzle

Questionnaire
Q & A session
Quiz show
Rap
Reader's theater
Rebus story
Recipe
Recipe book
Recommendation
Report
Research paper
Response paper
Riddle
Role-play
Schedule
Science fiction
Scrapbook
Script
Sculpture
Shoebox collection
Short story
Signs
Skit
Slide show
Slogan
Song
Speeches
Spelling bee
Sports story
Storyboard
Story poem
Story map
Summary
Survey
Tables
Tall tale
Timeline
Tri-fold
Venn diagram
Videotape
Weather report

Appendix J: Verbs to Question

The verbs listed below can be found on many different lists and are generally broken down into separate categories. It may be more useful to categorize them into just two alphabetized lists. The first list consists of verbs that are considered by most teachers to be lower-level recall verbs. The second list consists of verbs that are generally considered higher-order verbs.

LOWER-ORDER VERBS

add	infer
ask	interpret
choose	know
classify	label
compare	list
conclude	listen
contrast	locate
convert	match
count	memorize
define	name
demonstrate	observe
describe	omit
determine	outline
differentiate	paraphrase
discover	predict
discuss	read
display	recall
distinguish	recite
estimate	recognize
explain	record
express	relate
extend	repeat
find	rephrase
generalize	report
how	restate
identify	retell
illustrate	retrieve

review
rewrite
say
select
show
spell
state
summarize
tell

trace
translate
underline
what
when
where
which
who
why

HIGHER-ORDER VERBS

adapt
agree
analyze
apply
appraise
argue
arrange
assemble
assess
assume
award
build
calculate
categorize
change
classify
code
combine
compare
compile
compose
compute
conclude
connect
construct
contrast
convince
create
criticize
critique
debate

deduce
deduct
defend
delete
demonstrate
derive
design
determine
develop
diagnose
diagram
differentiate
discover
discriminate
dispute
dissect
distinguish
divide
draw
editorialize
elaborate
employ
examine
execute
experiment
explain
explore
formulate
hypothesize
illustrate
imagine

improve
infer
integrate
interpret
interview
invent
judge
justify
make up
manipulate
maximize
measure
minimize
model
modify
operate
order
organize
originate
paint
participate
perceive
perform
plan
practice
predict
prepare
pretend
prioritize
produce
propose
prove
rank

rate
rearrange
reason
recommend
reconstruct
record
relate
reorganize
revise
role-play
rule on
select
separate
sketch
solve
specify
state a rule
substitute
suggest
summarize
support
survey
teach
test
theorize
transfer
uncover
use
validate
value
verify
visualize
write

References

Anderson, T. H., & Armbruster, B. B. (1986). The value of taking notes during lectures (Tech. Rep. No. 374). Cambridge, MA: Bolt, Beranek and Newman and Center for the Study of Reading, Urbana, Illinois. (ERIC Document Reproduction Service No. ED 277 996).

Anderson, V., & Hidi, S. (1988/1989). Teaching students to summarize. *Educational Leadership, 46*, 26–28.

Armstrong, T. (2006). *The best schools: How human development research should inform educational practice.* Alexandria, VA: Association for Supervision and Curriculum Development.

Bond, G. W., & Smith, G. J. (1966). Homework in the elementary school. *The National Elementary School Principal, 45*(3), 46–50.

Bransford, J., Brown, A., & Cocking, R. (1999). *How people learn: Brain, mind, experience and school.* Washington, DC: National Academy Press.

Brookbank, D., Grover, S., Kullberg, K., & Strawser, C. (1999). Improving student achievement through organization of student learning. Chicago: Master's Action Research Project, Saint Xavier University and IRI/Skylight. (ERIC Document Reproduction Service No. ED 435094).

Cooper, H. (1989). Synthesis of research on homework. *Educational Leadership, 47*(3), 85–91.

Dale, E. (1969). *Audio-visual methods in teaching* (3rd ed.). Hinsdale, IL: Dryden Press.

Davis, O. L., & Tinsley, D. (1967). Cognitive objectives revealed by classroom questions asked by social studies teachers and their pupils. *Peabody Journal of Education, 44*, 21–26.

Duke study: Homework helps students succeed in school, as long as there isn't too much. (2006, March 7). Retrieved from http://today.duke.edu/2006/03/homework.html.

Education Northwest. (2005). Focus on effectiveness: Integrating technology into research-based strategies. Retrieved from Northwest Educational Technology Consortium website: http://www.netc.org/focus/.

Fillipone, M. (1998). Questioning at the elementary level. (Master's thesis.) Kean University. (ERIC Document Reproduction Service No. ED 417 431).

Fisher, D., & Frey, N. (2007). *Checking for understanding: Formative Assessment techniques for your classroom.* Alexandria, VA: Association for Supervision and Curriculum Development.

Fowler, T. W. (1975, March). An investigation of the teacher behavior of wait-time during an inquiry science lesson. Paper presented at the annual meeting of the National Association for Research in Science Teaching, Los Angeles. (ERIC Document Reproduction Service No. ED 108 872).

Janel W. (2009, October 18). Generating and testing hypotheses is not just for science [McRel blog]. Retrieved from http://mcrel.typepad.com/mcrel_blog/2009/06/generating-and-testing-hypotheses-is-not-just-for-science.html?cid=6a010536aec25c970b0115724ac441970b.

Johnson, D. W., & Johnson, R. T. (1999). *Learning together and alone: Cooperative, competitive, and individualistic learning.* Boston, MA: Allyn and Bacon.

Jones, F. A. (1908). *Thomas Alva Edison: Sixty years of an inventor's life.* New York: Thomas Y. Crowell.

Kagan, S., & Kagan, M. (1997). *Kagan cooperative learning smart card*. San Clemente, CA: Kagan Publishing.

Keith, T. Z., & Cool, V. A. (1992). Teaching models of school learning: Effects of quality instruction, motivation, academic coursework, and homework on academic achievement. *School Psychology Quarterly, 7*, 209–226.

Kuhn, M. (2009, June 22). Generating and testing hypotheses is not just for science [McRel blog]. Retrieved from http://mcrel.typepad.com/mcrel_blog/2009/06/generating-and-testing-hypotheses-is-not-just-for-science.html?cid=6a010536aec25c970b0115724ac441970b.

Lavoie, D. R., & Good, R. (1998). The nature and use of prediction skills in biological computer simulation. *Journal of Research in Science Teaching, 25*, 334–360.

Lawson, A. E. (1998). A better way to teach biology. *The American Biology Teacher, 50*, 266–278.

Leach, S. (2010, February 2). Generating and testing hypotheses is not just for science [McRel blog]. Retrieved from http://mcrel.typepad.com/mcrel_blog/2009/06/generating-and-testing-hypotheses-is-not-just-for-science.html?cid=6a010536aec25c970b0115724ac441970b.

Lehrer, R., & Chazen, D. (1998). *Designing learning environments for developing understanding of geometry and space*. Mahwah, NJ: Erlbaum.

Markman, A. B., & Gentner, D. (1996). Commonalities and differences in similarity comparisons. *Memory and Cognition, 24*(2), 235–249.

Marzano, R. J., Pickering, D. J., & Pollock, J. (2001). *Classroom instruction that works: Research-based strategies for increasing student achievement*. Alexandria, VA: Association for Supervision and Curriculum Development.

McGarvey, B. (2007, January). The war on homework. *Education Update, 49*(1), 6.

Meyer, B. F., & Freedle, R. O. (1984). Effects of discourse type on recall. *American Education Research Journal, 21*, 121–144.

National Council of Teachers of Mathematics. (2000). *Principles and standards for school mathematics*. Reston, VA: Author.

National Governors Association Center for Best Practices, Council of Chief School Officers. (2010). *Common core state standards for language arts*. Washington, DC: Author.

Pennsylvania Department of Education. (1973). *Study on homework: Homework policies in the public schools of Pennsylvania and selected states in the nation*. Harrisburg, PA: Author.

Redfield, D. L., & Rousseau, E. W. (1981). A meta-analysis of experimental research on teacher questioning behavior. *Review of Educational Research, 51*(2), 237–245.

Strang, R. (1975). *Homework: What research says to teachers* (Series). Washington, DC: National Education Association.

Vatterott, C., (2009). *Rethinking homework: Best practices that support diverse needs*. Alexandria, VA: Association for Supervision and Curriculum Development.

White, B. Y., & Frederickson, J. R. (1998). Inquiry, modeling, and metacognition: Making science accessible to all students. *Cognition and Instruction, 16*(1), 3–117.

About the Author

Michelle Manville taught elementary and middle school for sixteen years in Missouri and served as the K–12 curriculum director for her district for ten years. She also served on many local and state curriculum committees and was a Missouri Select Teacher for Regional Resources curriculum trainer for two years.

Since her retirement in 2010, Manville has written five resource books for teachers that identify specific, effective research-based strategies and activities. *Common Core State Standards for Grades K–1: Language Arts Instructional Strategies and Activities*, *Common Core State Standards for Grades 2–3: Language Arts Instructional Strategies and Activities*, *Common Core State Standards for Grades 4–5: Language Arts Instructional Strategies and Activities*, *Common Core State Standards for Grade 6: Language Arts Instructional Strategies and Activities*, and *Common Core State Standards for Grade 7: Language Arts Instructional Strategies and Activities* are available now. Grade 8 will be available soon.

Manville currently spends her free time with her husband on the family farm or at their home on Lake of the Ozarks.